D0932837

WAY
MORE
WEST

AND SELECTED POEMS NEW AND SELECTED POEMS NEW AND SELECTED
TED POEMS NEW AND SELECTED POEMS NEW AND SELECTED POEMS N

WAY MORE WEST

MS NEW AND SELECTED POEMS NEW AND SELECTED POEMS NEW AND
ND SELECTED POEMS

EDWARD DORN

INTRODUCTION BY DALE SMITH
EDITED BY MICHAEL ROTHENBERG

PENGUIN POETS

PENGUIN BOOKS
Published by the Penguin Group
Penguin Group (USA) Inc., 375 Hudson Street, New York, New York 10014, U.S.A.
Penguin Group (Canada), 90 Eglinton Avenue East, Suite 700, Toronto, Ontario, Canada M4P 2Y3 (a division of Pearson Penguin Canada Inc.)
Penguin Books Ltd, 80 Strand, London WC2R 0RL, England
Penguin Ireland, 25 St Stephen's Green, Dublin 2, Ireland (a division of Penguin Books Ltd)
Penguin Group (Australia), 250 Camberwell Road, Camberwell, Victoria 3124, Australia (a division of Pearson Australia Group Pty Ltd)
Penguin Books India Pvt Ltd, 11 Community Centre, Panchsheel Park, New Delhi - 110 017, India
Penguin Group (NZ), 67 Apollo Drive, Mairangi Bay, Auckland 1311, New Zealand (a division of Pearson New Zealand Ltd.)
Penguin Books (South Africa) (Pty) Ltd, 24 Sturdee Avenue, Rosebank, Johannesburg 2196, South Africa

Penguin Books Ltd, Registered Offices:
80 Strand, London WC2R 0RL, England

First published in Penguin Books 2007

10 9 8 7 6 5 4 3 2 1

LIBRARY OF CONGRESS CATALOGING IN PUBLICATION DATA
Dorn, Edward.
Way more West : new and selected poems of Edward Dorn / introduction by Dale Smith ; edited by Michael Rothenberg.
p. cm.—(Penguin poets)
Includes bibliographical references (p.   ).
ISBN 978-0-14-303869-6
I. Rothenberg, Michael. II. Title.
PS3507.O73277W38 2007
811'.54—dc22 2006050727

Printed in the United States of America
Set in Electra LH
Designed by Ginger Legato

Acknowledgments to Maya Dorn, Terri Carrion, Jane Dalrymple-Hollo, Anselm Hollo, Steve Fredman, Paul Slovak, and Yvonne Schofer, Humanities-English bibliographer at the Memorial Library, University of Wisconsin-Madison, and curator for the Sukov Collection of Little Magazines.

Special thanks to Jennifer Dunbar Dorn without whose editorial collaboration this collection would not have been possible.

—Michael Rothenberg

CONTENTS

EDWARD DORN: AN INTRODUCTION

No poet of the post-war era addressed the conflicting public interests of American democracy with the same rhetorical force as Edward Dorn. Whether he wrote with passionate lyricism or scathing satire, he always argued for the principles of locality against the self-interests often embedded in social and political abstractions. For him, more than most, poetry was written to reveal public situations many of us have experienced, such as July Fourth festivities, political election, and other civic incidents of custom. This public-mindedness influenced his work tremendously, and so the poems here, gathered from more than forty years of public engagement, reveal the praise and blame a poet may use to address his audience. He praised the weak and exploited laborers of the West and its native inhabitants while blasting with satirical invective those for whom power was a tool to extend self-interests. He also made himself accountable to his experience of the American West, relating it through his public and private uses of the poem.

Dorn grew up in the Midwest, a child of the Great Depression. The spirit of the small town and the farming communities rooted around it helped form his character. That world is at stake in early poems like "Are They Dancing," "The Air of June Sings," and "Sousa." He acknowledges with sympathy his "Time Wanderers" and the "forgotten places" where "the summer dresses of girls once blew." In the lyric sweetness of these poems, however—"the belief, the relief / of Sunday occasion"—he sees the grim conditions "of the deprived." He registers the economic and social forces that are thrust on people, like it or not, "without slipping into the mind-killing error of description." He does not offer solutions for poverty; he does not seek retribution for offenders of public faith. Instead he makes poetry that speaks through the present, praising those people who are rooted to the particulars of their experience, such as his own "forebears" who "owned a nice clapboard house" during the "intensity of the depression." His restless self-scrutiny extends an ethos in this early writing of insight and trepidation for the West he beheld:

> Yes, at moments I did waste
> our lives, giving way
> foolishly to public thoughts,
> large populations.

Are we needed? On this mountain
or in this little spud town in the valley
or along this highway, you held
your eyes on getting us there, repeatedly
where?

The concern for place and "public thoughts" gives these early poems a tension that will eventually find resolution in the great epic *Gunslinger*. What makes this early work significant, however, is a commitment to the New American writing of the 1960s, where social interrogation and self-scrutiny were related through a renewed lyric sensitivity. During this time, LeRoi Jones's Totem Press published *The Newly Fallen*. Other books from that pivotal decade of social confrontation include *Hands Up*, *Geography*, and *The North Atlantic Turbine*.

Prior to this prolific period of early writing, Dorn had begun attending Black Mountain College in North Carolina, where he studied with Charles Olson, Robert Creeley, and Robert Duncan. In *A Bibliography on America for Ed Dorn*, Olson outlined a course of study that would occupy Dorn's attention. Besides figures of literary modernism, Olson suggested readings from the philosophy of Alfred North Whitehead, the cultural geography of Carl Sauer, and the historical studies of the American West by Bernard DeVoto and Frederick Merk. By shifting stress from literature to the intersecting vectors of historical and geographic "fact," Olson insisted, "it is not how much one knows but in what field of context it is retained." Dorn's application of this bibliography led him to use the poem as a tool for discovery and judgment that is not based on aesthetic principles but on the organization of a field. In "The Problem of the Poem For My Daughter, Left Unsolved," he notes how "the oblivious process / of a brutal economic calculus" shifts his attention from "superficial . . . quality in other poems." He discusses this notion of a "field":

In the chronically vast complex
explanation, a field true,
but a field
no field hand knows
beyond the produce of it
on some citizen's land. . . .

The measure of his "field" against that of the "field hand" shows a tenuous link between poet and laborer. Dorn seeks a more permanent change in the process of how we think about the places we inhabit, and through the agency of the poem he arrives at a scathing list of the genetic and technological forces that leave a "man, / in that framed condition / of some totally onanized culture."

Gunslinger marks Dorn's radical departure from lyric to laughter—an un-avoidable release from the shock of the actual. Its epic narrative makes a meta-physical riot of Nixon-era public dialogue. While the poem focuses on the internal compositions and extensions of psychic forces at work behind Ameri-can social life, it is necessary to remember the intense turmoil of these years of war. The "Elizabethan ear" Robert Creeley admired in Dorn's early writing now tuned in on comic books, Westerns, drug slang, and slapstick to relate the more serious political and philosophical orientations of the West. This road trip epic stars a number of characters such as the transfigured "I" ("There will be some along our way / to claim I stinks"), the Gunslinger "of impeccable per-sonal smoothness," Dr. Flamboyant, and The Stoned Horse who rolls bomber joints. *Gunslinger* is an ironic and complex work that integrates humor and puns into its pre-Socratic revision of the Western psyche. As Michael Davidson has noted, "Dorn's Gunslinger is a problematic blend of existential outlaw, robber baron, and metaphysician," and through him "Dorn's view ranges over the en-tire industrialized world as a succession of replaceable parts in what he calls 'the cultural exchange.'" Conversations among key characters such as Lil and Kool Everything are often comedic and evasive in the poem's strategy of deflating the high tone of traditional epic. This is, however, a highly rhetorical work, with staged conversations and deliberations as the Gunslinger and his gang journey toward Four Corners, the geographic intersection where four Western states meet. Here, as in earlier poems, Dorn works against the progressive urgency of explanation:

> Questioner, you got some strange
> obsessions, you want to know
> what something means after you've
> seen it, after you've been there
> or were you out during
> That time? No.
> And you want some reason.
> How fast are you
> by the way? No local offense
> asking that is there?
> No.

The distinctions here are crucial to the underriding arguments of the book that suggest knowledge cannot be dumped into the brain as if it were some kind of container. Intent and instantaneous perceptions of experience create the only meaning we need. The time lag brought on by reflection and discursive lan-guage get in the way of speech, words, and actions. To get to this, "I" ("secretary to Parmenides") is Dorn's agent of change. After containment in a vat of LSD,

"I" emerges transformed as a kind of pre-Socratic new man, and he's got an an-
swer for any still in wait of one:

> Entrapment is this society's
> Sole activity, I whispered
> and Only laughter,
> can blow it to rags.

Gunslinger is essential today for its ex-static reading of The West. Its wit is timed
to imprint the more relevant dispositions of the Gunslinger and his crew deep in
the psyche of the reader. You hardly notice the draw as the bullet enters its tar-
get.

After the success of *Gunslinger*, Dorn turned increasingly to the epigram as
the prime literary form for his satirical attacks on public sensibility and the self-
interests of 1980s and '90s. In *Hello, La Jolla* and *Abhorrences* he aimed his in-
vective against European and American culture and its economic stranglehold
on world resources. He continued to view social problems, political greed, and
national aggression in genetic and technological terms. Unlike with *Gunslinger*,
the epigrams of *Hello, La Jolla* and *Abhorrences* offer poems that have been
stripped to a central message. The work inspires us to laugh, often uncomfort-
ably. For instance, in "Distraction Control" he says "The most oecological way /
to kill the fleas / is to kill the dog." Despite the surface plainness, these poems
often make insightful puns and redirect attention to show how the seemingly
mundane is completely significant. "One bullet," Dorn writes in *Abhorrences*,
"is worth a thousand bulletins." The pace in these epigrams is timed to deploy
maximum wit. Perspective is also important, for it is not a linear calculus by
which he moves his attention, but one of recurring pattern, so that, in "People of
the Earth," he says, "You should check your calculations. / From a distance, it
looks like / a chicken farm."

These poems are essential works of protest against what Dorn saw as an in-
creasingly apathetic public mind. Besides the policies and institutions he blasts,
his audience is often left to fend for themselves. It is not unusual to be made
uneasy by his views, but such challenges to sensibility lie at the core of Dorn's
late poetics. Like it or not, if you read him, you might be led into a kind of
awareness you had not anticipated. In "The Protestant View," for instance,
Dorn stresses the radical context of Protestant theology, forcefully stating "that
eternal dissent / and the ravages of / faction are preferable / to the voluntary /
servitude of blind / obedience." Such statements are insightful for their quick
connections of religious history to current situations where modern "consumer
societies" seem predicated by that unexamined servitude. This recognition of
the political force behind religious views would lead him to investigate the
Cathar heresy of twelfth-century France in his late work *Languedoc Variorum:*

A *Defense of Heresy and Heretics,* a poem sequence notable for its footnote-like "Subtexts & Nazdaks" that introduce a running commentary linking current social and political issues within the historical-poetic framework of the body of the main text.

Although the Taxol he was given to treat his cancer fuels *Chemo Sábe,* Dorn's last work, one poem in this collection relates a social and hereditary genealogy. "My tribe," he wrote, "came from struggling labor / Depression South Eastern Illinois / Just before the southern hills start / To roll toward the coal country. . . ." This deeply personal poem relates an unsettling geographic description of his people through the places they live and the work they do. It is also an indictment against the state. "Governments always conspire against / The population," he writes, "and often / This is not even malice; / Just nothing better to do." The final stanza identifies his American tribe with "every defiant nation this jerk / Ethnic crazy country bombs." "Tribe" is a public testament, a final relation of where he stands against state proposals of land division, political economy, social engineering, and ethnic chicanery.

Despite his force of opposition, the late poems seek a kind of redemption for human failing too, and share a sympathy for human struggles that he addressed earlier in his study of Apache resistance, *Gran Apachería,* and in the poems of protest he translated from the Spanish with Gordon Brotherston, *The Sun Unwound.* Dorn finds through the harrowing composition of *Chemo Sábe* strength in the lyric's mediation of personal urgency to protest his cancer. In "The Garden of the White Rose," where "mercy is stretched so thin / to accommodate the need / of the trembling earth," he wonders how he can find relief for his "singularity," observing "the White Rose, whose / house is light against the / threatening darkness." These tensions of public testament and private vision give *Way More West* an astonishing edge, relating the insight of his "singularity." His attention to place and people come together here with biting wit, and also love. For a tenderness and vulnerability to public inspection mark these poems as uniquely his own. Think of them as communications across the great distance of the West.

Dale Smith
Austin, Texas

WAY
MORE
WEST

The Rick of Green Wood

In the woodyard were green and dry
woods fanning out, behind
                              a valley below
a pleasure for the eye to go.

Woodpile by the buzzsaw. I heard
the woodsman down in the thicket. I don't
want a rick of green wood, I told him
I want cherry or alder or something strong
and thin, or thick if dry, but I don't
want the green wood, my wife would die

Her back is slender
and the wood I get must not
bend her too much through the day.

Aye, the wood is some green
and some dry, the cherry thin of bark
cut in July.

My name is Burlingame
said the woodcutter.
My name is Dorn, I said.

I buzz on Friday if the weather cools
said Burlingame, enough of names.

    Out of the thicket my daughter was walking
singing—
         backtracking the horse hoof
    gone in earlier this morning, the woodcutter's horse
    pulling the alder, the fir, the hemlock
    above the valley
               in the november

air, in the world, that was getting colder
as we stood there in the woodyard talking
pleasantly, of the green wood and the dry.

                      1956

Vaquero

The cowboy stands beneath
a brick-orange moon. The top
of his oblong head is blue, the sheath
of his hips
is too.

In the dark brown night
your delicate cowboy stands quite still.
His plain hands are crossed.
His wrists are embossed white.

In the background night is a house,
has a blue chimney top,
Yi Yi, the cowboy's eyes
are blue. The top of the sky
is too.

The Hide of My Mother

1

My mother, who has a hide

on several occasions remarked what
a nice rug or robe
my young kids would make,

Would we send them to her?
When we had them butchered?

It was certainly a hoo ha ha
from me
and a ho ho
from my wife: and I would amusedly say
to conceal the fist in my heart
which one? the black?

or the grey
& white?

And she would smile, exposing the carnival
in her head

What's the difference, after they're dead?

Can you imagine asking a poet that?
Perhaps I should tell her about my pet rat.

2

My mother remarked
that in Illinois

little boys sell holly
from door to door,

and *here*, she would say
they grow all over the mountains

what if I took a holly tree back
there? would it grow?
No. I said.

3

Once my mother
was making dinner

and my cats were on the floor.

Why do they whine like that?
she asked,

why don't we throw them all out the door?
why don't you feed them I ventured?

She said she wasn't indentured.

Can you imagine telling a poet that?
Later she fed them my pet rat.

4

One day my son
found a parakeet in the bush
brought it to the house
carrying the little blue thing by the tail.

My mother said why, isn't it pretty,
I wonder if it would make the trip home
to Illinois. Oh, I said, we'll have to find its owner

you don't want to pull a boner
like that.

5

Tho winter's at term
it still gets cold

in the evening.

My pets are warm

because I have set a fire.

My mother is arranging some ferns
and young trees, a little too big

she found in the mountains.
A jig, of a sort must be going

on in her head. It is raining
outside. Do you think I can get the copper legs

of that stool in the box
or is it too wide? With some of those

pretty rocks I saw on the beach, would you,
she was saying to my little boy,

like to go home to Illinois with grandmother?

He was saying from inside the box enclosure,
he wasn't sure he

wanted to leave his mother.

6

For a point of etiquette,
when I observed she was digging
the neighbor's English Privet,

I said, it grows in abundance here.

As a matter of fact, she had it,
I thought I saw a rabbit,
that's why I came over here.

I said, a plant like that might grow anywhere.

Well now, I suppose you are right
back home our elms have the blight

but the land is flat there
so many mountains hereabouts

Yes, I allowed, it must help the sprouts . . .

Well now, there's more rain here
than we have in Illinois in an entire year
wouldn't you think tho it would grow there?

I said, what about a Privet hedge from . . .

You remember the peonies on grandfather's grave
well someone took them they were gone
the last Memorial Day I was there.

. . . From Hudson's Bay to the Gulf of Carpentaria.
Do you think it would stay?

Oh I love plants but where I am the weather
drives the birds away.

7

As for the hides of other people,
My wife told her

of how the junkman's
woman had been so good to us

a truss as it were, had kept the children
when it was a hardship

the condition had been foul, sleet,
masses of air, a raw affair,

dumped out of the Yukon upon
us, roving bands of weather

sliding across British Columbia
a kind of dementia

of the days, frozen water pipes

and the wringer on the washing machine

busted, no coal.
Our house split in two like Pakistan.

The graciousness
of the woman of the junkman

she said. Now what do you think
we should do? forget it? some doughnuts?
a cake?

"Why, I don't know what I would do"—
my mother was alluding

to a possible misfortune of her own.

8

As for the thick of it,
really, my mother
never knew about the world.

I mean even that there was one,
or more.

Whorled, like a univalve shell
into herself,

early to bed, nothing
in her head, here and there
Michigan one time,   Ohio
another. Led a life
like a novel, who hasn't?

As for Sociology:
garbage cans were what she dumped
the remains of supper in,

dirty newspapers, if blowing
in the street, somebody probably

dropped them there.

Nobody told her about the damned
or martyrdom. She's 47

so that, at least, isn't an emergency.

Had a chance to go to Arizona once
and weighed the ins and outs

to the nearest ounce:
didn't go. She was always slow.

Incidently, for her the air
was Red one time:

tail end of a dust storm
somehow battered up from Kansas.

1957

Are They Dancing

There is a sad carnival up the valley
The willows flow it seems on trellises of music
Everyone is there today, everyone I love.

There is a mad mad fiesta along the river
Thrilling ladies sing in my ear, where
Are your friends, lost? They were to come

And banjoes were to accompany us all
And our feet were to go continually
The sound of laughter was to flow over the water

What was to have been, is something else
I am afraid. Only a letter from New Mexico
And another from a mountain by Pocatello.

I wonder, what instruments are playing
And whose eyes are straying over the mountain
Over the desert
And are they dancing: or gazing at the earth.

The Air of June Sings

Quietly and while at rest on the trim grass I have gazed,
admonished myself for having never been here
at the grave-side and read the names of my Time Wanderers.
And now, the light noise of the children at play on the inscribed
    stone

jars my ear and they whisper and laugh covering their mouths.
    "My Darling"
my daughter reads, some of the markers
reflect such lightness to her reading eyes, yea, as I rove
among these polished and lime blocks I am moved to tears and
    I hear
the depth in "Darling, we love thee," and as in "Safe in Heaven."

I am going off to heaven and I won't see you anymore. I am
going back into the country and I won't be here anymore. I am
going to die in 1937. But where did you die my Wanderer?
You, under the grave-grass, with the tin standard whereat
I look, and try to read the blurred ink. I cannot believe
you were slighted knowing what I do of cost and evil
yet tin is less than granite. Those who buried you should have
    known
a 6 inch square of sandstone, flush with the earth
is more proper for the gone than blurred and faded flags.

Than the blurred and faded flags I am walking with in the
    graveyard.

Across the road in the strawberry field two children are stealing
their supper fruit, abreast in the rows, in the fields of the overlord,
Miller his authentic name, and I see that name represented here,
there is that social side of burial too, long residence,
and the weight of the established local dead. My eyes avoid
the largest stone, larger than the common large, Goodpole
    Matthews,
Pioneer, and that pioneer sticks in me like a wormed black cherry
in my throat, No Date, nothing but that zeal, that trekking
and Business, that presumption in a sacred place, where children
are buried, and where peace, as it is in the fields and the country
should reign. A wagon wheel is buried there. Lead me away

to the small quiet stones of the unpreposterous dead and leave
me my tears for Darling we love thee, for Budded on earth and
   blossomed
in heaven, where the fieldbirds sing in the fence rows,
and there is possibility, where there are not the loneliest of all.

Oh, the stones not yet cut.

1958

Geranium

I know that peace is soon coming, and love of common object,
and of woman and all the natural things I groom, in my mind, of
faint rememberable patterns, the great geography of my lunacy.

I go on my way frowning at novelty, wishing I were closer to home
than I am. And this is the last bus stop before Burlington,
that pea-center, which is my home, but not the home of my mind.
That asylum I carry in my insane squint, where beyond
the window a curious woman in the station door
has a red bandana on her head, and tinkling things hand themselves
to the wind that gathers about her skirts. Oh in the rich manner
of her kind
she waits for the bus to stop.   Lo, a handsome woman.

Now, my sense decays, she is the flat regularity, the brick
of the station wall, is the red Geranium of my last Washington stop.
Is my object no shoes brought from india
can make exotic, nor hardly be made antic would she astride
a motorcycle, (forsake materials and we shall survive together)
nor be purchased by the lust of schedule.

No,

on her feet therefore, are the silences of nothing.   And leather
leggings adorn her limbs, on her arms are the garlands of ferns
come from a raining raining forest and dripping lapidarys dust.
She is a common thief of fauna and locale (in her eyes
are the small sticks of slender land-bridges) oh a porter
standing near would carry her bundle, which is scarlet too,

as a geranium and cherishable common that I worship and that I sing
ploddingly, and out of tune as she, were she less the lapwing
as she my pale sojourner, is.

Sousa

Great brass bell of austerity
and the ghosts of old picnickers
ambling under the box-elder when the sobriety
was the drunkenness. John,

you child, you drumhead, there is no silence
you can't decapitate
and on forgotten places (the octagonal
stand, Windsor, Illinois, the only May Day
of my mind) the fresh breeze
and the summer dresses of girls once blew
but do not now. They blow instead at the backs
of our ears John,
under the piñon,
that foreign plant with arrogant southern smell.
I yearn for the box-elder and its beautiful
bug, the red striped and black-plated—
your specific insect, in the Sunday after noon.

Oh restore my northern madness
which no one values anymore and shun,
its uses, give them back their darkened instinct
(which I value no more) we are
dedicated to madness that's why I love you
Sousa, you semper fidelis maniac.

And the sweep
of your american arms
bring a single banging street in Nebraska
home, and your shock
when a trillion broads smile at you
their shocking laughter can be heard long after
the picnickers have gone home.

March us home through the spring rain
the belief, the relief
of occasion.

Your soft high flute and brass
remind me of a lost celebration I can't

quite remember,
in which I volunteered as conqueror:
the silence now stretches me
into sadness.

Come back into the street bells
and tin soldiers.

                *   *

But there are no drums
no drums, loudness,
no poinsette shirts,
there is no warning, you won't recognize anyone.

Children and men in every way
milling, gathering daily, (those vacant eyes)
the bread lines of the deprived are here
Los Alamos, 1960, not Salinas
not Stockton.

Thus when mouths are opened,
waves of poison rain will fall, butterflies
do not fly up from any mouth in that area.

                *   *

Let me go away,
shouting alone, laughing
to the air, Sousa be here
when the leaves wear
a blank radio green, for honoring without trim
or place.

   To dwell again in the hinterland
and take your phone,
play to the lovely eyed people in the field
on the hillside.

Hopeful, and kind
merrily and possible
(as my friend said, "Why can't it be

like this all the time?"
her arms spread out before her).

        *   *

John Sousa you can't now
amuse a nation with colored drums
even with cymbals, their ears
have lifted the chalice of explosion
a glass of straight malice, and
we wander in Random in the alleys
of their longfaced towns taking
from their sickly mandibles handbills
summoning our joint spirits.

I sing Sousa.

The desire to disintegrate the Earth
is eccentric,
And away from centre
nothing more nor sizeable
nor science
nor ennobling
no purity, no endeavor
toward human grace.

        *   *

We were
on a prominence though
so lovely to the eye eyes
of birds only caught
all the differences
of each house filled hill.

And from the window a spire
of poplar, windows
and brown pater earth buildings.

My eye on the circling bird

my mind lost in the rainy hemlocks of Washington
the body displaced, let it
wander all the way to Random and dwell
in those damp groves
where stand the friends
I love and left: behind me
slumbering under the dark morning sky

are my few friends.

Oh, please
cut wood to warm them
and stalk never appearing animals
to warm them,
I hope they are warm tonight—
bring salmonberries
even pumpkinseed.

Sousa,
it can never be
as my friend said
"Why can't it be like this all the time?"
Her arms spread out before her
gauging the alarm,
(with that entablature)
and the triumph of a march
in which no one
is injured.

Like a Message on Sunday

Sits
   the forlorn plumber
by the river
with his daughter
   staring at the water
then, at her
his daughter closely.

Once World, he came
to our house to fix the stove
           and couldn't
 oh, we were arrogant and talked
about him in the next room, doesn't
a man know what he is doing?

Can't it be done right,
    World of iron thorns.
Now they sit by the meagre river
by the water . . . stare
into that plumber
so that I can see a daughter in the water
she thin and silent,
he, wearing a baseball cap
   in a celebrating town this summer season
may they live on

on, may their failure be kindly, and come
in small pieces.

Prayers for the People of the World

They were an exercise the ages go through
smiling in the church one time
banging and blowing in the street another
where brother is a state very often of glue
coming apart in the heat
of British Guiana where
the drainage and open canals
make difficult the protection of the lower classes
who have lands and moneys, food and shelter
in the great escrow called Never.

Though black cuban beards and armored cars shout contrary.

Did America say give me your poor?
Yes for poor is the vitamin not stored
it goes out in the urine of all endeavor.
So Poor came in long black flea coats
and bulgarian hats
spies and bombers
and she made five rich while flies covered the rest
who were suppressed or murdered
or out-bred their own demise.

If it should ever come

And we are all there together
time will wave as willows do
and adios will be truly, yes,

 laughing at what is forgotten
and talking of what's new
admiring the roses you brought.
How sad.

You didn't know you were at the end
thought it was your bright pear
the earth, yes

another affair to have been kept
and gazed back on
when you had slept
to have been stored
as a squirrel will a nut, and half
forgotten,
there were so many, many
from the newly fallen.

Home on the Range, February, 1962

Flutes, and the harp on the plain
Is a distance, of pain, and waving reeds
The scale of far off trees, notes not of course
Upon a real harp but chords in the thick clouds
And the wind reaching its arms toward west yellowstone.
Moving to the east, the grass was high once, and before
White wagons moved
                the hawk, proctor of the hills still is

Oh god did the chunky westerner think to remake this in his own
    image
Oh god did the pioneer society sanctify the responsible citizen
To do that
         face like a plot of ground
Was it iron locomotives and shovels were hand tools
And barbed wire motives for each man's
Fenced off little promised land

                or the mind of bent

    Or of carson, oh earp
    These sherpas of responsible destruction

Posses led by a promising girl wielding a baton upon the street
A Sacagawea wearing a baseball cap, eating a Clark bar.
And flutes and the harp are on the plain to
Bring the last leading edge of stillness
Brought no water, brought dead roots
Like an allotment of tool handles to their premises—and they cry
In pain over daily income—a hundred years of planned greed
Loving the welfare state of new barns and bean drills
Hot passion for the freedom of the dentist!
Their plots were america's first subdivisions called homesteads

Lean american—gothic quarter sections gaunt look
Managing to send their empty headed son who is a ninny
To nebraska to do it, all over again, to the ground, a prairie
Dog hole,
And always they smirk at starvation
And consider it dirty . . . a joke their daughters learn
From their new husbands.

On the Debt My Mother Owed to Sears Roebuck

Summer was dry, dry the garden
our beating hearts, on that farm, dry
with the rows of corn the grasshoppers
came happily to strip, in hordes, the first
thing I knew about locust was they came
dry under the foot like the breaking of
a mechanical bare heart which collapses
from an unkind an incessant word whispered
in the house of the major farmer
and the catalogue company,
from no fault of anyone
my father coming home tired
and grinning down the road, turning in
is the tank full?   thinking of the horse
and my lazy arms thinking of the water
so far below the well platform.

On the debt my mother owed to sears roebuck
we brooded, she in the house, a little heavy
from too much corn meal, she
a little melancholy from the dust of the fields
in her eye, the only title she ever had to lands—
and man's ways winged their way to her through the mail
saying so much per month
so many months, this is yours, take it
take it, take it, take it
and in the corncrib, like her lives in that house

the mouse nibbled away at the cob's yellow grain
until six o'clock when her sorrows grew less
and my father came home

On the debt my mother owed to sears roebuck?
I have nothing to say, it gave me clothes to
wear to school,
and my mother brooded

   in the rooms of the house, the kitchen, waiting
for the men she knew, her husband, her son

from work, from school, from the air of locusts
and dust masking the hedges of fields she knew
in her eye as a vague land where she lived,
boundries, whose tractors chugged pulling harrows
pulling discs, pulling great yields from the earth
pulse for the armies in two hemispheres, 1943
and she was part of that *stay at home army* to keep
things going, owing that debt.

Los Mineros

Now it is winter and the fallen snow
has made its stand on the mountains, making dunes
of white on the hills, drifting over
the flat valley floors, and the cold cover
has got us out to look for fuel.

Has got us first to Madrid which is 4 miles beyond Cerillos
close to the Golden Mountains
a place whose business once throve like the clamor in Heorot Hall;
but this was not sporting business, The Mine Explosion of 1911.
And on the wall in the mine office

                          there in Madrid

are two pictures of those blackbirds, but a time later;
the thirties, and the bite of the depression is no bleaker
on their faces than is the coming morning of the day they were took.
These men whom we will never know are ranged 14 in number
in one of those pictures that are very long, you've seen them.

And the wonder is five are smiling Mexicanos, the rest
could be English or German, blown to New Mexico on another
winter's snow. Hard to imagine Spanish as miners, their
sense is good-naturedly above ground (and their cruelty).
In a silly way they know their pictures are being taken,

and know it isn't necessary honor standing in line with their hands
    hiding
in their pockets. I was looking to see if they are short
as Orwell says miners must be, but they aren't save two
little Mexican boys.   What caught my eye at first was the way
they were so finely dressed in old double-breasted suit coats, ready
    for work.

Then I looked into their faces and the races separated.
The English or Germans wear a look which is mystic in its expectancy;

able men underground,
but the Spanish face carries no emergency

and one of the little boys, standing behind a post
looks right out of the picture faintly smiling: even today. Martinez
whom I had gone with was waiting for the weight slip.
When we got over to the giant black chute the man above waved
as from the deck of a troubled ship and said no carbon
amigos, and then climbed down the ladder.

Madrid is a gaunt town now. Its houses stand unused
along the entering road, and they are all green and white,
every window has been abused with the rocks of departing children.

In My Youth I Was a Tireless Dancer

But now I pass
graveyards in a car.
The, dead lie,
unsuperstitiously,
with their feet toward me—
please forgive me for
saying the tombstones would not
fancy their faces turned from the highway.

Oh perish the thought
I was thinking in that moment
Newman Illinois
the Saturday night dance—
what a life!   Would I like it again?
No.   Once I returned late summer
from California thin from journeying
and the girls were not the same.
You'll say that's natural
they had been dancing all the time.

Hemlocks

Red house.   Green tree in mist.
How many fir long hours.
How that split wood
warmed us.   How continuous.
Red house.   Green tree I miss.
The first snow came in October.
Always.   For three years.
And sat on our shoulders.
That clean grey sky.
That fine curtain of rain
like nice lace held our faces
up, in it, a kerchief for the nose
of softest rain.   Red house.

Those green mists rolling
down the hill.   Held our heads
when we went walking on the hills
to the side, with pleasure.
But sad.   That's sad.   That tall grass.
Toggenburg goat stood in, looking, chewing.
Time was its cud.   Oh
Red barn mist of our green trees of Him
who locks our nature in His deep nature
how continuous do we die to come down
as rain; that land's refrain
no we never go there anymore.

From Gloucester Out

It has all
come back today.
That memory for me is nothing
there ever was,
                    That man

so long,
when stretched out
and so bold
                on his ground
and so much
lonely anywhere.

But never to forget
                    that moment

when we came out of the tavern
and wandered through the carnival.
They were playing
the washington post march
but I mistook it for manhattan beach
for all around were the colored lights
of delirium
                to the left the boats
of Italians
and ahead of us, past the shoulders
of St. Peter the magician of those fishermen

the bay
stood, and immediately in it the silent
inclined pole where tomorrow the young men
of this colony
so dangerous on the street
will fall harmlessly
into the water.

They are not the solid
but are the solidly built
citizens, and they are about us

as we walk across
                    the square
with their black provocative
women
slender, like whips of
sex in the sousa filled night.

Where edged
by that man in the music
of a transplanted time and
enough of drunkenness
to make you senseless of all
but virtue
                    (there is never
no, there is never a small complaint)
(that all things shit poverty,
and Life, one wars on with
many embraces) oh it was a time that was perfect
but for my own hesitating
to know all I had not known.
Pure existence, even in the crowds
I love
will never be possible for me

even with the men I love
                    This is
the guilt
that kills me
          My adulterated presence

but please believe with all men
I love to be

          .   .

That memory
of how he lay out
on the floor in his great length
and when morning came,
late,
we lingered
in the vastest of all cities

in this hemisphere
                    and all other movement
stopped, nowhere
else was there a stirring known to us

yet that morning I stood
by the window up 3 levels
and watched a game
of stick ball, thinking of going away,
and wondering what would befall that man
when he returned to his territory.
The street as you could guess
was thick with their running
and cars,
themselves, paid that activity
such respect I thought a ritual
in the truest sense,
where all time and all motion
part around the space of men
in that act
as does a river flow past
the large rock.

        •   •

And he slept.
in the next room, waiting
in an outward slumber
                    for the time

we climbed into the car, accepting all things
from love, the currency of which is
parting, and glancing.

Then went
out of that city to jersey
where instantly we could not find our way
and the maze of the outlands west
starts that quick
where you may touch
your finger to liberty
and look so short a space

to the columnar bust
of New York
and know those people exist
as a speck in your own lonely heart
who will shortly depart,
taking a conveyance for the
radial stretches
past girls on corners
past drugstores, tired hesitant
creatures who I also love
in all their alienation were it not so
past all equipment of country side
to temporary homes
where the wash of sea and other
populations come
once more to whisper only one thing
for all people: a late and far-away
night yearning for
and when he gets there
I want him to stay away
from the taverns of familiarity
I want him to walk by the seashore alone
in all height
which is nothing more than
a mountain. Or the hailing of a mast
with big bright eyes.

So rushing,
          all the senses
come to him
as a swarm of golden bees
and their sting is the power
he uses as parts of
the oldest brain. He hears
the delicate thrush
of the water attacking
He hears the cries, falling gulls
and watches silently the gesture of grey
bygone people. He hears their cries
and messages, he never

ignores any sound.
As they come to him he places them
puts clothes upon them
and gives them their place
in their new explanation, there is never
a lost time, nor any inhabitant
of that time to go split by prisms or unplaced
and unattended,
                        that you may believe

is the breath he gives
the great already occurred and nightly beginning world.
So with the populace of his mind
you think his nights? are not
lonely. My God. Of his
loves, you know nothing and of his
false beginning
you can know nothing,
                        but this thing to be marked
again

          only

he who worships the gods with his strictness
can be of their company
the cat and the animals, the bird he took
from the radiator
of my car saying it had died
a natural death, rarely seen in a bird.

To play, as areal particulars can out of the span
of Man, and of all, this man

does not
          he, does, he
      walks
                by the sea
in my memory

and sees all things and to him
are presented at night
the whispers of the most flung shores
from Gloucester out

[1964]

FROM
GEOGRAPHY

Song: The Astronauts

for clair oursler

On the bed of the vast promiscuity
of the poet's senses is turned
the multiple world, no love is possible
that has not received the
freight of that fact
no wake permissible that has not met
the fluxes of those oceans.
the moon orbits
only for that permission.
Men with fine bones in their heads
will manipulate a recovery
and put spades into her
only to find Euripides went before them
            the hymen long ago fixed
it is an old old wedding
but as you dig you will not hear
the marriage flutes
you will be killed in your sleep.
Broken.
you will be considered pirates

and killed when Hymenaeus
(who lost his voice and life
                    singing at a wedding
catches you asleep
in the rushes of
the windless moon

              the immensely soft glow of it
              will always be behind you
              as you stand on its face
                             staring
                    at the strangely
              inhabited world
                             from whence you came
              from where all men with their eyes
              have been satisfied

                    before thee

The Problem of the Poem for My Daughter,
Left Unsolved

The darkness rings.
                    the surface form
      of the face, a halo
of the face,
as it passes away in the air as she moves
   between the buildings, a cut
   surrounding her throat, the pearls
   of the price she'll never have to insist
she paid
         a thin line red with its own distinction
some goiter
of what she has been made to understand is civilization
not the brand of the adventurous cutlass

The misery is superficial now.
I have dwelt on that quality in other poems
without attention to the obvious
drain
      of social definition
the oblivious process
of a brutal economic calculus, where to
                   place the dark hair
save above moist eyes
the black slacks,
the desperately optimistic rouge of the fallen cheeks
                  (cheeks are up
when they live
     both forward *and*
posterior, the colorado of new day not a new state . . .
where the leads are I despair to find lead mines

          In the chronically vast complex
explanation, a field true,
but a field
no field hand knows
beyond the produce of it
   on some citizen's land, the horizons
sheer the top

of the head of the man
    who is bent
bent is an attitude
    I've settled on now
        to define a man
  whose attention is forced down
a class, distracted, not a stratum
detained from what the reaper called attention
    might harvest, O false shift of season
in a vacation
           but how slow, and seasonal
    and the poem is an instrument of intellection
    thus a condition
    of the simultaneous
    so the woman and myself, pass,
    and her message bears a huge meanness
        "the measureless crudity of the States"

A world where no thing thrives short of the total pestilence
of its spirit, and because there is no intelligence short
of the total there is no intelligence, none. There is not even one
intelligence in the land, children see the capitol of things
shifted to disneyland, no misery
which does not know all misery,
as an eye of knowledge, contrary to happiness
that quite exclusive short range and burst, as it happens
a birthday party, my daughter's. I had gone to the supermarket
for ice cream.   and saw the shocked woman

    We call the intersection of time
and event the
devastation of a fortune cake
all answers pulled out
of the standard of living which is that cake
no standard is cake
a provided nation
is no standard, rather a thorn
in the side of a more careful world
    her pain affirmed (all men and women
who suffer deeply, in any way, are not
cannot be U.S. Citizens, no matter where
they live. They may live in Indiana

she carried no standard,
        as I saw her: impossible to be a citizen
        there is no such thing anywhere, in any country.
    I could have shot her down, had she been a marine.
    She was a housewife.

And leaving the scene, and the legal questions
not one male canaanite would have come forward
She was no phœnician raped broad,
there are never any ships parked by the bannock county court house
this woman was sometime willingly captured by another,
a sort of community, her husband, if she is unfortunate enough to
                                                    possess one

is probably a masonic reservist.

        No woman is Helena
unless the culture has provided for the passage of pain
and no people can construct the delicacies of culture
until they imagine Helena, merely fucking in the middle
of the atlantic on the SS United States is not it, is procurement
while the full-sized poodle whines in the kennel above
back of the forward stack, the echo of the sound he makes in Berkeley
where the hippest member of the minority group as it was reported
arrived in a sports car and there it was, white, with a beret
wearing shades, sitting beside the driver, looking with disdain
on a small cur who trotted along the curb and stopped
for one brief moment of curiosity and then resumed
his policing of the bases of parking meters

        These United States.
have sent forth women, hopeless divorcees,
the wrinkled millionairesses of resources dwindled
to a day dream, the exhausted mesaba of their dangling breasts
soft wax structures to support our collectively ceaseless greed
for legitimate youth, but divided states do not create women,
Amelia Earhart
was not carried off, she flew, like something familiarly
transvestite in us, a weirdly technical Icarus
she was sent for by some morse-code spiritism, this land
was never more than the bitter hardness of nouns for us
her destiny was not qualified by myth
                        She came in all her beauty

to a small green island
in a bag of metal, oh misfortune that to be exemplary is so difficult
she could have been a goddess because she flew, other women
marked by sex, fold out of the minds of american men
who may no longer wear the bottoms of their trousers rolled
but who are certainly all circumcised without ritual
and wear the ends of their penises rolled
and always assure their dentists they are masturbators:

                                         the paraphernalia
of an existence, thus a human phenomenon, culture-less
(pop culture,
              technologically provisioned
(those are collections of people grasping nothing
                                    the women are
                            set loose to walk spiritless
their marks are deep cuts on the neck, moist eyes, sagging nylons
eyes painted to dry everything, loose figures of despair
or hard flesh prolonged by injections and tucks into an isolated youngness
a manufactured Galateability
                                    The end
                                    of applied genetics will be
                                    the elimination of freely disposed
                                    intellection, via the rule
                                    that a science is oriented toward
                                         Use, some predictable
                            breed, is the end
(Automation ends with a moral proposition, THE LESSON of
one maximum factor of it
will suggest all the correspondences:
                                    mail food ads
                                    the attractive stuffing
                                    from McCalls and House Beautiful
                                    to Havana
                                         during any season
              of famine, therefore those people will hunger more
(which people?
the natural seedbed of that morality
is plague, and all such endeavor
instructs one to move our daughters
to some green island
in the sea, we are so far from Galilee

The sum of her
shall perish, has begun
to perish in the darkside
in the prescribed field of misery
and she will hardly avoid the destruction
of her nature,
a material of birth
as a car of new life
   not new, novel, the life
   is older than that we know as prima materia
      And soon when there is no need
for waitresses, or telephones, doctors' wives
and automobilists, they wither
on their still green vine, no more tears
to water life, no more varicose veins
the Kaddish will be said
not as a formal memory
but for the working of a curse, venus
will be likewise a disease transmitted for a secure experience
a memory of Eve for some isolated engineer
who said if I don't do it, someone else will
      A man,
      in that framed condition
      of some totally onanized culture, who will
      transmit with the bills of requisition
      the bill that held Leda off the ground
      in that throbbing moment when she saw histories of the future
      in the bright feathers, knew the spines of
      that ancient creature in her thighs

   the engineer's note:
Send me a little syphilis this month,
                              I have been reading
                                 some old books

and in that sense
there is no loss to *a* man
of his earlier knowledge,
a yawn simply defines the brink of availability:
                        Hello there Ed, congratulations!
                        I've forgotten the *details*
                        but it sounded *fabulous*!

It is the night of the opening
of the new art-grocerystore and all the shoppers
were discussing theology, a science which has no subject-matter,
something about the indistinguishability of environment where all
the mistakes of logic create a different object, something
without tears, something

          as I get it less like
          the terrestrial entry a cave or
          less similar volcano than woman
          something omitting holes
          a specifically anti metaphorical being
          like a man protruding, an extension
          no intention, space is still not conceived
          (as surrounding: infinity is the inability
          to conceive, the collapse
          of surrounding,
          female principle was structure
          before and somewhat after the opening
          of the art-grocerystore

So tears, or the rose enfolds
the moisture of its passion
the girl my daughter, 14 today
and such eyes, all interior, a proud thing
born in 1951, not yet bestowed with any curse, she is
Chansonette, a woman, hopefully, for nomads
a principle older than man, a running out
the tear dropped into an earth rapidly drying tonight,
the disappearance instant
into the most unimaginable laundromat, the danger
a wholly adjectival father might worry over
in the nest of the most corrupted notion thus far: America!
of how men might, if they were noble
behave in their last moments we barely speak
except for the relatively sour hope that some nineteenth century
and romantically singular form of bloodletting
be reinstated because the man in the street hears a choir
of pioneers' voices and thinks of brigadiers when a rightist is hurt
where he sits on the porch of his finca faraway

                    or of how we might
plead our case in the face of Sartre's observation
that this is a nation where those who care

are the damned of the earth, *running* I will add
before the furious nations who snap at our heels
with a momentum of the centuries, and I stand
behind the pane at my window one of those hopeless men, some silly

                                                    toscanini

leading the symphony
in the street, directing the movements, I do so know
all the scores by heart, by a memory
saturated with defeat, where crisis and alienation
are no more new than any other condition but were always
bred in this strewn and used land, no cultural tricks of assimilation
to form a cover,

                  bunchgrass is an isolated cover,
has a slight brief flower,
and I can tell my daughter no secret.

West of Moab

The caravan wound. Past the pinto bean capitol
of the world and mesa verde.
Bitterly cold were the nights.
The journeymen slept in the lots of filling stations
and there were the interrupting lights
of semis all night long as those beasts
crept past or drew up to rest their motors
or roared on.

A modern group in cars.
They travelled north at an angle
and the tired engines whirred
moreso the rear plant of the nazi car
from the strain of the great
american desert. Past places
they went, like only mormons
and in Green River
they had coffee and talked to an old woman
whose inconsistency was radical
so demented was she
by the isolation of the spot and the terrible dry winds
that blow down upon south Utah.
and what she had to ward them off
were not the slow dreams of indians
but a pool table and a rack of cold sandwiches.

The beer was cold
The four sat and drank.
Hot, the climate was tolerable only
within the confines of bars or on
the open stretches of road at mad speed
or at night when the bitter cold sat over the southern
Colorado cliffs.

In the bitterness of the great desert
they tried to get comfortable in car seats.
Utterly left behind was
a mixed past, of friends and a comfortable house.

They felt sorry for themselves perhaps
for no real reason, there had never
been in their baggage more than a few stars
and a couple of moons, you've seen their surfaces
in pictures.
They came finally to the brick facade
of salt lake & much beyond. A year later
those who remained celebrated—
almost as an afterthought, and remembered
that day it snowed when they left,
September 1st . . . now it is October
and winter has not yet sent her punitive expedition.
Warm days. It is afternoon. The leaves
come and go in the Alberta wind sliding down
across our country
and they sit still facing the north slopes
of the mountains, the remnant of a Southern Idea
in their minds.

Idaho Out

For Hettie and Roi

> "The thing to be known is the natural
> landscape. It becomes known through
> the totality of its forms"
>
> Carl O. Sauer

1

Since 1925 there are now no
negative areas he has ignored
the poles have been strung for our time together
and his hand is in the air as well

areal is hopefully Ariel

     So black & red simplot fertilizer smoke

drifts its excremental way
down the bottle of our
valley
toward the narrowing
end

coming into the portneuf gap
where its base aspects . . .
a large cork could be placed
but which proceeding from inkom

               or toward

past the low rooves
of sheep's sheds the slope
gains rough brusque edges
and you are in it more quickly
than its known forms allow

    or the approach from
the contrary side of the valley

there is a total journal
with the eyes
and the full gap stands
as the grand gate from our
place
to utah bad lands and
thus down
to those sullen valleys
of men who have apparently
accepted all of the vital
factor of their time
not including humanity.

     And not to go too far with them
they were the first white flour makers

               they jealously
keep that form and turn the sides
of the citizens' hills into square documents
of their timid endeavor. The only
hard thing they had was first massacre
and then brickwork
not propaedeutic to a life of grand design
wherein *all* men fit
                    but something
for all its pleasure of built surface
and logic of substances as
the appeal of habitat
     for salt lake downtown is
     not ugly,
     but to a life of petty retreat
     before such small concourses
     as smoking, drinking, and other less
     obvious but
     justly necessary bodily needs
     not including breeding which in their hands
     is purposive.

From this valley
there is no leaving by laterals.
Even george goodhart,

a conventional man, as all
good hearts are
knew, with a horse
and access crosswise
to creekheads
the starving indian women could be fed
with surplus deer.
Who was the pioneer boy who died in a rest home
and was a new local, i.e.,
there is implied evidence
he never heard the cry of the pawnee
in his territory.
Which, it is said in the human
ecology term
is to be a hick, howsoever travelled. And
while we are at it it is best said here:

The mark of the pre-communication
westerner
travelled in local segments
along a line of time
utterly sequestered
thus his stupidity required the services
of at least one of his saddle bags
and, in the meantime
his indian friends
signalled one another over his head
as he passed on his businesslike way
in the depressions
between them, in long shadows
they looking deaf and dumb, moving fingers
on the slight rounds
of nebraskan hills.

Of a verge

of the land North
and an afternoon is no good
there is the width of the funnel rim
and sad people for all their smiles
do scurry and sing across its mouth
and there are no archipelagoes of real laughter

in alameda
and no really wild people save stiff
inhibited criminals.
So when gay youth was yours
in those other smaller towns on the peneplain
of central america and the jerseys
the white legs of girls stand truly by stoplights
and Edward Hopper truly did stop painting
all those years. But we stray
we strays, as we always do
and those mercies always wanted

an endless price, our jazz came
from the same hip shops we walked past
the truly, is no sense speaking of universes,
hanging from that hook

       I had in mind the sweet shop
something so simple as main street
and I'll be around.

But I was escorting you out of Pocatello,
sort of north.
Perhaps past that physiographic
menace the arco desert and
what's there
of the leakage of newclear seance

          to Lemhi
again a mormon nomenclature
where plaques to the journey of Lewis & Clark
but the rises across the too
tilted floors of that corridor
at high point the birch
and then toward North Fork
you must take that
other drainage where yes
the opposites are so sheer
and the fineness of what growth
there is that lifting
            following
of line, the forever bush

and its thin colored sentinelling
of those streams
                        as North Fork comes on
on the banks of the magnificent salmon
we come smack up on a marvelous beauty from Chi.

    Who has
a creaky cheap pooltable
to pass the winter with
and the innocent loudmouthed handsome
boys who inhabit the
winter there. The remarkably quiet winter
there,
all alone where the salmon forks.
It is so far away but never long ago.
You may be sure Hudson.
And
She said
shaking her dark hair
she used to work at arco
and knew the fastest way
from salmon to idaho falls—
you may be sure
and in a car

                or anywhere,

she was a walking invitation
to a lovely party
her body was that tactile to the eye
or what I meant
she is part
of the morphology
the last distant place of idaho north,
already in effect Montana.
Thus, roughly free,
to bring in relative terms.
Her husband, though it
makes no difference,
had sideburns, wore
a kind of abstract spats

wore loose modern beltless pants
and moved with that accord to the earth
I deal with
but only the heavy people
are with.
　　They are "the pragmatic 'and'
the always unequated remnant"

　　2

My desire is to be
a classical poet
my gods have been men . . .
and women.
I renew my demand
that presidents and chairmen everywhere
be removed to a quarantine outside the earth
somewhere,
as we travel northward. My
peculiar route is across
the lost trail pass past
in the dark draws somewhere
my north fork beauty's husband's
dammed up small dribbling creek

fetching a promising lake (she showed
me the pictures) a too good to be true
scheme she explained to me,
to draw fishermen with hats on
from everywhere
they wanted to come from.
One of the few ventures I've
given my blessing . . . she
would look nice rich.

　　3

We were hauling . . .
furniture. To Missoula.
We stopped in the biting
star lit air often to have

a beer and to stretch our legs.

My son rode with me
and was delighted that a state
so civilized as Montana
could exist, where the people,
and no matter how small
the town,
and how disconnected in
the mountain trails,
could be so welcoming to a lad,
far from the prescribed ages
of idaho where they chase that
young population out, into
the frosty air. There is
an incredible but true fear
of the trespassing there of such
patently harmless people aged 13.

But not to go too much into
that ethnic shit, because
this is geographic business,
already, in the bitteroot
there sat snow on the tallest
peaks and that moisture factor
caused trees now gliding by
from one minor drainage
to another until we came
to the great bitteroot
proper and the cotton woods
and feather honey locusts
lining its rushing edges.
Once, when I was going the other way
in august,
a lemhi rancher
told me the soil content
of the bitteroot was of
such a makeup that the cows
got skinnier whereas
in the lemhi, you know
the rest, although of course
the lemhi is dry. It's

like a boring popular song
all by himself he'd love
to rest his weary head
on somebody else's shoulder
as he grows older.

From Florence to Missoula
is a very pragmatic distance
And florence is the singularity
Montana has, one is so drunk
by that time. Fort Benton,
to your right, across stretches
of the cuts of the Blackfoot, through
Bowman's Corner, no
the sky

is not

bigger in Montana. When
for instance you come
from Williston
there seems at the border a change
but it is only because man has
built a tavern there
and proclaims himself of service
at a point in time, very much,
and space is continuous from Superior
to Kalispel. And indeed

That is what the dirtiest
of human proportions are built on
service by men there before you

could have possibly come
and you never can.

But if men can live in Moab
that itself is proof nature
is on the run and seeding very badly
and that environmentalism, old word,
is truly dead.

4

So he goes anywhere apparently
anywhere and space is muddied
with his tracks
for ore he is only after,
after ore.
He is the most regretful factor
in a too miniscule cosmic
the universe it turns out your neighbors are

The least obnoxious of all
the radiating circles bring
grossnesses
that are of the strength of bad dreams.

5

Let me remind you we were in Florence
Montana.
Where the Bitteroot is thick
past Hamilton, a farm machinery
nexus
for all that unnutritious hay
and in florence we stop.

Everyone gets out of the trucks
and stretching & yawning moves
through the biting still starlit night
a night covered with jewels
and the trucks' radiators begin
to creak and snap in their cooling off.

We shiver. Each limbjoint
creaks and shudders and we talk
in chatters of the past road, of the failing
head lights on the mountain road—and in
we go.

A wildly built girl
brushes past us
as we enter. Inside

it is light, a funny disinherited place
of concrete block. The fat woman
bartender,
has an easy smile as we head for the fireplace
in the rear and as we go by the box is putting out
some rock and twist, and on the table
by the fireplace there are canned things, string beans
and corn, and she brings us the beer.

Florence. It is hardly a place.
To twist it, it is a wide spot
in the valley. The air is cold. The fire
burns into our backs while we sit on the hearth.
The girl of the not quite
believable frame
returns, and her boyfriend is pulled
by the vertically rhythmic tips of her fingers
reluctantly off the stool,
but he can't
he, the conservative under riding buttress
of our planet can't, he has been drinking beer
while she, too young for a public place
has been pulling a bottle apart in the car.

So there you are. She is
as ripe and bursting as that
biblical pomegranate.
She bleeds spore in her
undetachable black pants
and, not to make it seem too good
or even too remote
or too unlikely near
she has that
kind of generous smile
offset by a daring and hostile look
again, I must insist, her hair
was black, the color of hostile sex
the lightest people, for all
their odd beauty,
are a losing game.

. . . I can't leave her.
Her mother was with her.
She, in the tavern, in Florence
was ready,
with all her jukeboxbody
and her trips to the car
to the bottle.
There are many starry nights thus occupied
while the planet, indifferent, rattles on
like the boxcars on its skin
and when moments like that transpire
they with all good hope begin again somewhere.
She made many trips to the car that night . . .
an unmatchable showoff
with her eyes
and other accomplishments.

6

And onward
bless us, there are no eyes
in Missoula, only things, the new
bridge across Clark Fork
there is civilization again,
a mahogany bar
                    and tickertape

baseball, and the men are men,
but there are no eyes
in Missoula
like in little orphan annie and is?
the sky bigger there?

        The sky disdains
to be thus associated and treacherous cowboys
who drive cars live there.
Say the purity of blue over Houston
that unwholesome place
is prettier
and the graininess over Michoacan is moodier
and I have been to wyoming.

7

The trip back sadly as all trips
back are
                    dull
and I did
see the old bartender woman of florence
this time in her restaurant part 50 yards
away from the tavern between which
she ran apparently with the speed
of some sort of stout gazelle
but not the broad with the fabulatory build.
She that day was probably off in an office somewhere.
Pity daytime lives.
But everyone was tired. We had unloaded
the furniture, early the next morning
and before the bite of the sun quelled the bite
of the stars we left, going the long, time consuming
way
south. Sober business.
The Beauty of North Fork was there as she will be
till she dies sometime
(and by the way she runs a tavern)
Thence to salmon and across the narrow bridge
and out
into the lemhi. I say
if it weren't for the distances
and for the trees & creeks I would
go mad, o yes, land, that one forces
a secondary interest in, vanishes
as a force as you drive onward.
This is only obvious.
This is only some of the times we spend.
You go through it as though it were
a planet of cotton wadding . . . and love
its parts as you do the parts of a woman
whose relations with earth are more established
than your own.

But of physical entirety
there is no need to elaborate, one has
one's foot

on the ground, which is the saying
of all common and communicable pleasures
and my arm around your shoulder is the proof of that.
But I am ashamed of my country
that, not as areal reality, but as act
it shames me to be a citizen in
the land where I grew up. The very air chills
your bones, the very ungraciousness of its replies
and the pressures of its not replying
embarrass my presence here. God knows
we do what we can to live.
But the intimidations thrown at us
in the spurious forms they have learned truth
can take, in a time which should have been
plenty and engaging of the best that each man,
if he were encouraged to be even that, and
not slapped in the face as stupid, cut off
from all other peoples to make him hygienic of
views not viable to this soil, which is no more
sacred I tell you than any other the earth
has to offer, for she in her roundness has kept
an accord with her movements great time has not yet
seen aberrant. Mice crawling on a moving body?
can they, may they really offset great movement?

The very air,
if you are awake, can chill your bones
and there is little enough of beauty
finally scratched for. It is not
the end pursuit of my countrymen
that they be great
in a great line of men.
An occasional woman, won't,
though I wish she could,
justify a continent. In the parliaments
of miniscule places she is there
and gives them substance,
as in Florence, and North Fork
for she was gracious as leaders
are now not and I begin to believe after all
these years there *is* an aristocracy
of place and event and person

and as I sit here above this valley
I sought to involve you with
and take you out on a trip
that had no point, there remains Montana
        and it is nice. But not infallible.
The sky is a hoax.
And was meant,
once suggested,
to catch your eye. The eye
can be arbitrary,
but its subject matter cannot.
Thus the beauty of some women.
And from Williston
along the grand missourian length
of the upper plains you go, then the Milk
to Havre
that incredible distance once along a route
all those clamorous men
took . . . they now grow things there not horticultural
only storageable, things of less importance
than fur
for furs then were never stockpiled, it would
hurt the hair,
                that Astor,
he'd never have done it.

And yes Fort Benton is lovely
and quiet, I would gladly give it as a gift
to a friend, and with pride, a place of marked
indolence, where the river closes, a gift
of marked indifference, if it were mine.
If the broad grass park were mine
between the river and the town
and to the quick rise behind.
And then up to the median altitude of Montana
Sugar beets and sheep and cattle.

Where the normal spaces
are the stretches of Wyoming
and north Dakota, Idaho
is cut
by an elbow

of mountain that swings
down, thus she is
cut off by geologies she says
I'm sure
are natural
but it is truly the West
as no other place,
ruined by an ambition and religion
cut, by a cowboy use of her nearly virgin self

       unannealed
by a real placement
             this,

this
is the birthplace
of Mr. Pound
and Hemingway in his own mouth
chose to put a shotgun.

Song

This afternoon was unholy, the sky
bright mixed with cloud wrath, I read Yeats,
then black, and their land of heart's desire
where beauty has no ebb
$$\text{decay no flood}$$
but joy is wisdom, time
an endless song
$$\text{I kiss you}$$
and the world begins to fade
I kiss you not, the world is not.
I would not give my soul to you yet
the desire inside me burns.
November. The eighteenth was the coldest
this season, encumbered with routine errands
out past the factory
$$\text{black sulphur}$$
and in the dense checks
of its burdensome smoke the intense yellow tanks,
hooded, there sat a smell of weak death

and we pass these days of our isolation
in our rigidly assigned shelters
heads bent in occupation
a couple of pointless daydreamers
smiles lit and thrown into the breeze,

how artful can love
suffer in the cross streets of this town
marked simply by the clicking railroad
and scratch of the janitor's broom.

Song

Christ of the sparrows Help me!
    the soot falls
        along the street
  into the alleys.
december.

and sometimes
    its rain falls
      along pocatello's streets
    into its alleys
    along its black diesel thruways

There is no far away place
could satisfy
there is no forlorn bird
could outdistance my desire.
When the vacation
of my heart is that complete
the pain of this
particular moment
is unbearable. The sun
strikes my book laden table
my room is my skull
I could have you tell me
this pain behind my eyes will soon be gone
I could listen, I could die
seized by a foolishly contrived misunderstanding

or listlessly watch
    the two single
figures bent
and in the rags of careful hesitation
feel their way along the sidewalk
past my window
old men
leave a city already made lonely
by the outcast words of pointless conversation
    go,
along the intolerably windy highway west of here.

        And mind us
there were no marks of the bruise of friends
there aren't any traces of that turmoil, you stay

as you were, there were
a few headlong pitches onto the ground
a torn shoulder to remember
a few unhappy nights.
drunk with the high necessity to talk
fast and loud in crowded bars
And then, in the street
to spit silently out
the cheap guilt
and all the casual half meant and self aware
inward chastisement
a petty reward for myself, like saving a nickel
and insisting even with a smile
it was *my* life I lived
the suspicious terror I'd turned around
too many times to keep track
I said you said I said You said I said.

The Smug Never Silent Guns of the Enemy

Their muzzles are at the door.
Did you see them, did he
see them, minutemen
rising out of the silos
A winter wonderland of
the white busy north.
The smug guns, trained on
The whites of their eyes
are grey
          and disputations
of more guns come
into the ear:
   The manipulated price of sugar
   The death of great ladies
   "I'll shoot my second if you'll shoot yours"
   Concentrated insecticides
   (flow like milk in the river
   You will be greeted
   on the outskirts of town
   with a vegetable brush
   and tips on good living
   An interview with a turkey farmer
     (gobbling in the background
the news that Bertrand Russell
   is a sick old fool
   The seminar ends when the squat madeyed colonel
   announces the way to peace thru war and shoots the moderator

And more corrupted reports follow you out
the door, they implore you to think young
and you do
it is such a pleasure in the sagebrush
in the open saturated air
zipping up your pants
having made more of the latest news
on the new snow.

Mourning Letter, March 29, 1963

No hesitation
                would stay me
from weeping this morning
for the miners of Hazard Kentucky.
                The mine owners'
extortionary skulls
whose eyes are diamonds don't float
down the rivers, as they should,
of the flood

            The miners, cold
starved, driven from work, in
their homes float though and float
on the ribbed ships of their frail
bodies,

            Oh, go letter,
keep my own misery close to theirs
associate me with no other honor.

Song: Venceremos

(for latin america
(for préman sotomayor

And there will be fresh children once more
in planalto and matto grosso
green mansions for their houses
along the orinoco
     take away the oil
     it is not to anoint their heads
     take away the cannon
     and the saber from the paunch belly
     overlaid with crossed colors
     those quaint waddling men
     are the leaden dead toys
                   only their

           own
         children

           caress
     while the great eyed children
     far away in the mountains, out of Quito
     pass thru the crisp evening streets
     of earth towns, where they caress
     the earth, a substance of *majority*
     including the lead of established
     forces,
who can do nothing
     but give us the measures of pain
         which now define us

Take away the boats from the bananas
they are there for the double purpose
to quell insurrection first
and next to make of an equatorial food
a clanging and numerical register in chicago
this is not industrial comment,
it is not Sandburg's chicago
not how ugly a city you did make
but whitman's fine generosity I want
a specific measure of respect returned for the hand
and the back that bears away the stalk

as a boy, in illinois
peeled away, in amazement, the yellow, brown lined case
                                                     thicker place

when the arced phenomenon
was first put in his hand
a suggestion and a food, combustion!
keep your fingers from the coffee bush.

                                         Nor,
on the meseta Basáltica, or back in town
in Paso de Indios
can the people be permitted
the luxurious image of Peron
and his duly wedded saint
they can be taught to deny
the dictator and his call girl
in the sports car
hide themselves in some corrupt
rooming house country
with a blue coast
and damned clergy

                "memory, mind, and will
                  :politics
          "there are men with ideas
           who effect"

Force those men.
be keen to pass beyond all known use
use the grain on a common mountain
for those who are hungry
                         treat hunger
as a ceremony
be quick to pass by condition
and the persuasion of mere number
        teach the parrot, who rises
                in the sunset
           a cloud
        to sing,
destroy
        all talking parrots
     I ask you

make for the
                altar
        of your imaginations

        some sign   Keep
    the small clerks of God from your precinct
be not a world, and therefore halt
before the incursions of general infection
                from a stronger world,
            dance,
                    and in your side stepping
        the spirit
            will tell where.

Song: Europa

Red wine will flow
sadly past your lips, and leave
with fullness their parting
october is orange
with desolation
the mountains are abandoned
each winter sunset
to those cruel marks of red
or whole lines of remote ranges
lit of desire for you as they recede
                              toward oregon

Nothing will happen.
The brutality of your frankness
has come to me
inches at a time,
and so slowly the pain marches
through the veins of my soul
with the heavy step of a migrating herd
tramping out the vintage
Evening is
              that closing part
of you I sometimes hum as a song to myself
looking down the street through my fingers
through the wreath of myrtle
                         with which you have embellished
                                   my horns

I call
with the thick weight
in my throat
over your terrain
                 O she is a small settlement, there
she is an atmosphere
and we are above it all
under her white gown

and against my bare shoulder
snow flakes fall
a slight scent of ginger
fresh in the wind
of our trip to Knossos

For the New Union Dead in Alabama

The Rose of Sharon
      I lost in the tortured night
  of this banished place
   the phrase
    and the rose
     from wandering
away, down the lanes
   in all their abstract directions
    a worry about the peninsula
  of the east,
     and the grim territories
        of the west
      here in the raw greed
     of the frontier my soul can find
   no well of clear water
    it is pressed
  as a layer
    between unreadable concerns,
      a true sandwich, a true
    grave, like a performance
      in an utterly removed theater
    is a grave, the unreachable action makes
    a crypt
       of distance,
  a rose of immense beauty
    to yearn for,
         the cutting of it
    cutting off the world
    the thorn however
 remains, in the desert
 in the throat of our national hypocrisy
   strewn we are along all the pathways
of our exclusively gelding mentality
      we stride in
       our gelding culture,
   oh rose
     of priceless beauty

refrain from our shores
suffocate the thin isthmus
of our mean land,
cast us back
into isolation

FROM
THE NORTH ATLANTIC TURBINE

Thesis

Only the Illegitimate are beautiful
and only the Good
proliferate only the Illegitimate
Oh Aklavik only you are beautiful
Ah Aklavik your main street is dead
only the blemished are beautiful only
the deserted have life made
of whole, unsurpassable night
only Aklavik is life inside life inside
itself.
They have gone who walk stiltedly
on the legs of life. All life is
in the northern hemisphere turning around
the radicals of gross pain and great joy
the poles of pure life move
into the circle of
our north, oh Aklavik only
the outcast and ab
andoned to the night are faultless
only the faultless have fallen only
the fallen are the pure Children of the Sun
only they move West, only they are expected,

in the virgin heat
    by those who wait intensely
  for the creatures from the East, only
Aklavik, our Aklavik, is North
    and lovely, always abandoned
   always dark, whose warp is light.
Simple fear compels Inuvik, her liquor store
     lifts the darkness
   by the rotation of a false summer.
The Children of the Sun never go
 to Inuvik, on bloody feet, half starved,
or suffering the absolute intrusion
   of any food oh Aklavik they vomit
on your remote and insupportably obscure streets
which run antiseptically into the wilderness
 and if blackflies inhabit with the insistence
of castanets the delta of Inuvik in you Aklavik
 around you Aklavik they form a core
   and critical shell of inflexible lust, only
 in the permafrost
    is the new home of the Children
 of the Sun in whose nakedness
   is the desire not desire
  in whose beauty is the flame of red
permafrost a thousand feet deep in whose
   frail buildings
    the shudder of total winter in whose
  misshapened sun the Children bathe

On the Nature of Communication, September 7, 1966

As Dr. Verwoerd one day
sat at his appointed desk
in the parliament at Capetown
there came to him a green
and black messenger.
(who did not, in fact, disagree with him)

and Dr. Verwoerd looked up
as the appropriately colored man
approached. He expected
a message. What he received
was a message. Nothing else.

That the message was delivered
to his thick neck
and his absolute breast
via a knife,
that there was a part tied
to the innate evil of the man
is of no consequence
and as the condolences, irrelevant.

Thus, in the nature of communication
Dr. Robert Kennedy is deeply shocked
and Dr. Wilson shocked
Dr. Portugal, that anonymous transvestite
is "with" the gentle people of
South Africa in this their moment
            of grief
            and wishes them well

in their mischief. A practical
and logical communication. Pope
Johnson also deplored etc.
Dr. Mennen Williams said something about "africa".

By its nature communication
ignores quality and opts for accuracy:

come on, tell us how many nigger's balls
tonight. Do not fold bend spindle or mutilate,
I needn't tell anyone
who has received a paycheck,
is each man's share in the plan.

Wait by the door awhile Death, there are others

Is this the inch of space in time I have
I awoke just now
I don't know from what
I could suppose a certain gas
                it could have been
      thinking of myself

Is this thing made
with the end built-in
the component of death hidden only
in the youthful machine
but discoverable if the wrench
                of feeling
is turned near forty when the doors
shut with a less smooth click
and biological delinquescence
a tooth broken and unrecoverable
ah news from the Great Manufacturer.

This afternoon someone, an american
from new york, spoke
to me knitting his brows, of
"the american situation" like
wasn't it deplorable, a malignancy
of the vital organs say News
from nowhere. A mahogany sideboard of tastes.
I knitted my brows too
an old response
      and tried to look serious
Look like I was thinking of quote back home.

Look like I *have* a home, pretend
like anyone in the world
I know where that is. And could
if I chose, go there.

I thought sure as hell
he is going down
the whole menu

          Civil rights cocktail
          Vietnam the inflexible entree

oh gawd what will there be for pudding
(not another bombe

I shifted deftly out the window
of the new university, the english workers
saunter easily building this thing.

      What has been my stride
My body remains younger
than I am. I let part of my beard grow
in September and touching it
with my hand when I turned in bed
I woke up. Hair on the face is death
it is that repels the people gets
a sociological explanation. Disaffection
is in our day the fear of death
the bare face is thought permanent,
a rock. But not clean.
The cat is cleaner when he licks
his hair and claws following a meal.

I nearly died the other day, without intention.
And when I thought Death had come for me
before My Time I was in a fright
to know what to do last
in what city to meet my gunner Meg
be beside me
                and laughed
like a tired runner at the end of hurrying.
                It was dry.
The laughter a hiss at environment.
And just now, reconsidering this
I hear the crows, I have
not seen augurous birds since we moved
away from the rookery in Lexden churchyard
they rise with the dawn now and flutter
in hoarse astonishment
around the top of the sycamore in the garden
the mists from the North Sea move rapidly by.

The wind rushes and turns. "A blackening train
Of clamorous rooks thick urge their weary flight.

I have no more sense of death than
the imitations the starlings
bring and no cold wish to be there
in that place. The rot of finger tips
and an old fern grown full inside my skull
are the passing, dull
presentments I have.
I have felt already the reality
of the last breath I draw in.
I want to say something.
           I want to talk
turn myself into a tongue

It was a short exhalation
rose from me as the smoke
from a blown out candle
thick with the first vacuum
then suddenly thin, the intention
of a whisper and smile.

The question of the child
"what is it" is only possible
from the neuter distance of the child
when a stranger walks alone
far out on the quay
or, as there are no estuaries
where I come from
across an open field

The crossection of the monument of Death
involves the shadow of
the rushing spider
when it is crushed
but the intersection of the moon
is absolute
  the human presence
    and the power to be
    is that small
  our time and

                place
                   is that limited
                         our cry for god
         that weak
               our religion
                     that constructed

There was a Saturday gathering
of people
Stones outside shop near Pound's
london residence, Kensington walk
a mews. My dream
had me pound stone. A woman agent
of the university of texas was there
didn't meet her, and another awful creature

from new york.
We drank small glasses of bubbly wine
said to be from Spain, tasting suspiciously
morocco. Headstone.

                   How we inscribe our days
to boredom. The next week I sat
while a harmless collagist
drew my portrait.
But I was bored past the threat of
Death. It took a double shot of whiskey
in Liverpool street to revive me.

It is difficult enough to sit still for love
and now the price of the time for that
rises like the hem, or goes down
as some predictable opposite. April
is my month, I learn the 6th card
of the major arcana. But so is March
the zodiac cuts me that way, the ram
and the bull, it is love I am
or the 5th, and mediate the material
and divine, a simple sign   the ram
the reflection of Isis. I wear
a tiara. I can think of people
who won't believe that.

                    The body. I am
however, the host of my body.
I invite myself to enter myself.
I have gone there sometimes with great pleasure.

        We are not in God's name. At the end,
when the dreaming of the dream
came I "thought" I was Sophia Loren
a mature venus. I don't resemble her.
She could be Mama Courage.

In God's name I do not seek an end.
The imitation of life is more vivid
                than life
                        (Paul, here is your
                                name
                        as cool as anything

So there is a dream story
    of a true enough man named Pedro
"a man without a country"
in the cowering simplicity of the newspaper phrase
it is reported he was a stowaway
on the English cargo ship Oakbank 2 years ago
but he has no papers and every country
rejects him. He says he is Brazilian.
He will ply the seas, a captive there
until he dies. His references do not exist.
No Deans will welcome him. No housewives
have come forth with a cup of coffee
no workers will welcome him upon the job
no greeting of any kind seems forthcoming.
He shall ply the seas until he dies.
His references do not exist. Notice.
No one will recommend him. His first name
is all he has, always the sign of
an acutely luckless man, his first name
can be used by anyone, indeed only
his first name, the excuse for abandoning him
is complete. Even the crew of the Oakbank
I should imagine
are waiting for the day he, idling about the ship

washes over and saves them the handling
of his body against the rail and into the foam
where he at last must be and even now is
as he walks the decks, no nation possesses
the apparatus to fix another identity
or any identity for this man who is without one.
He is the man we all are and yet he doesn't exist.
He is the man we would all save with our tongues
because we are secretly him. His references of course
do not exist. He may recall as we do
the uncertain days on shore
when they did, when once, remember that time
the world seemed open what a satisfying meal
that was. The body outlives
in Pedro too, its lighted parts. The rest
is application, qualified and eager young man
or woman, fluent french and english
would travel . . .

A Notation on the evening of November 27, 1966

The moon is a rough coin tonight
full but screened by lofty moisture
bright enough to make sure
of the addresses
on the letters I drop in the red pillar box
Frost is on the streets. A soft winter breeze
comes from the North Sea into my nostrils
I am at home here only in my mind
that's what heritage is.
Turning the corner, only our windows
along the ribbon of road are lit
I know my wife has gone to bed
and that the gas is burning
and that my heart and my veins
are burning for home. Yet those abrupt times
I hear the harsh voice of home
I am shocked, the hair on my neck
        crawls.
This evening we all went to see
an old classic flick at the Odeon.
The magnificent seven introducing
Horst Buchholst, I'd seen it before
and *had not* got it that a german
played a mexican, of course!
An American foreigner is every body
navajoes play iroquois
the American myth is only "mental" a foreigner
is *Anybody*. Theoretically at least
an Italian could play
an English man or a London jew

if nobody knew.
Tom and Jenny were there
and Nick Sedgwick.
Tom remarked, on the evidence of
the last scene when the Mexican-
Japanese said Vaya con Dios
and Yul said a simple adios,
"that was philosophical."

Then the five of us went home
singing Frijoles!
twirling our umbrellas
and walking like wooden legged men in a file
one foot in the gutter
        the other on the sidewalk.

Song

Again, I am made the occurrence
Of one of her charms. Let me
Explain. An occupier
Of one of the waves of her intensity.

        One meeting

Behind the back
      of the world
Brief and fresh
And then
Nothing.
Winter nights
The crush of fine snow
A brilliancy of buildings around us
Brief warmth
In the cold air, the cold temperament
Of a place I can't name

    Now what is it. Turning into
A shadowed corridor half the earth away
And deep inside an alien winter
I remember her laugh
The strange half step she took

       And I would not believe it
If Europe or England
Could in any sense evoke her without *me,*
The guitar of her presence the bearer of her scent
Upon my wrist
The banding of her slightsmiling lassitude . . .

The Sundering U.P. Tracks

(the end of the North Atlantic
 Turbine poem

I never hear the Supremes
but what I remember Leroy.
McLucas came
to Pocatello the summer of 1965
one dark night he was there
in a brilliant white shirt, one
dark evening the U.P.
brought him, the most widely luminous
and enchorial smile
       I ever saw.
               He had taken rooms
with the Reverend Buchanan
over in that part of town owned
by Bistline, the famous exploiter.

I was hurt to discover he had come
to what I thought was my town in my fair country
three days before. I had thought
he would stay with me.
How many thousand years too late now
is that desire. How long will the urge to be
remain. Every little bogus town
on the Union Pacific bears the scar
of an expert linear division.

           The rustic spades
           at the Jim Dandy Club
           took his money
           like sea winds lift
           the feathers of a gull
     "Compared to the majestic legal thievery
of Commodore Vanderbilt men like Jay Gould
and Jim Fisk were second-story workers . . ."

     (rest comfortably Daniel Drew)

Each side of the shining double knife
from Chicago to Frisco
to Denver, the Cheyenne cutoff
the Right of Way they called it
and still it runs that way
right through the heart
the Union Pacific rails run also to Portland.
Even through the heart of the blue beech
hard as it is.

                    2000 miles or so
                each hamlet
            the winter sanctuary
                    of the rare Jailbird
                and the Ishmaelite
            the esoteric summer firebombs
        of Chicago
                the same scar tissue
            I saw in Pocatello
        made
        by the rapacious geo-economic
        surgery of Harriman, the old isolator
        that ambassador-at-large

You talk of color?
Oh cosmological america, how well
and with what geometry
you teach your citizens

FROM GUNSLINGER

Book I

The curtain might rise
anywhere on a single speaker

for Paul Dorn

I met in Mesilla
The Cautious Gunslinger
of impeccable personal smoothness
and slender leather encased hands
folded casually
to make his knock.
He would show you his map.

There is your domain.
Is it the domicile it looks to be
or simply a retinal block
of seats in,
he will flip the phrase
the theater of impatience.

    If it is where you are,
the footstep in the flat above

in a foreign land
or any shimmer the city
sends you
the prompt sounds
of a metropolitan nearness
he will unroll the map of locations.

His knock resounds
inside its own smile, where?
I ask him is my heart.
Not this pump he answers
artificial already and bound
touching me
with his leathern finger
as the Queen of Hearts burns
from his gauntlet into my eyes.

  Flageolets of fire
he says there will be.
This is for your sadly missing heart
the girl you left
in Juarez, the blank
political days press her now
in the narrow adobe
confines of the river town
her dress is torn
by the misadventure of
    her gothic search

The mission bells are ringing
in Kansas.
Have you left something out:
Negative, says my Gunslinger,
no *thing* is omitted.
Time is more fundamental than space.
It is, indeed, the most pervasive
of all the categories
in other words
theres plenty of it.
And it stretches things themselves
until they blend into one,
so if youve seen one thing

youve seen them all.

I held the reins of his horse
while he went into the desert
to pee. *Yes*, he reflected
when he returned, that's less.

How long, he asked
have you been in this territory.

Years I said. Years.
Then you will know where we can have
a cold drink before sunset and then a bed
will be my desire
if you can find one for me
I have no wish to continue
my debate with men,
my mare lathers with tedium
her hooves are dry
Look they are covered with the alkali
of the enormous space
between here and formerly.
Need I repeat, we have come
without sleep from Nuevo Laredo.

And why do you have such a horse
Gunslinger? I asked. Don't move
he replied
the sun rests deliberately
on the rim of the sierra.

And where will you now I asked.
Five days northeast of here
depending of course on whether one's horse
is of iron or flesh
there is a city called Boston
and in that city there is ahotel
whose second floor has been let
to an inscrutable Texan named Hughes
Howard? I asked
The very same.
And what do you mean by inscrutable,

oh Gunslinger?
I mean to say that He
has not been seen since 1833.

But when you have found him my Gunslinger
what will you do, oh what will you do?
You would not know
that the souls of old Texans
are in jeopardy in a way not common
to other men, my singular friend.

You would not know
of the long plains night
where they carry on
and arrange their genetic duels
with men of other states—
so there is a longhorn bull half mad
half deity
who awaits an account from me
back of the sun you nearly disturbed
just then.
Lets have that drink.

STRUM

strum

      And by that sound
we had come there, false fronts
my Gunslinger said make
the people mortal
and give their business
an inward cast. They cause culture.
Honk HONK, Honk HONK Honk
that sound comes
at the end of the dusty street,
where we meet the gaudy Madam
of that very cabaret going in

where our drink is to be drunk—
        Hello there, Slinger! *Long time*
no see
what brings you, who's your friend,
to these parts, and where
if you don't mind my asking, Hello,
are you headed . .

Boston!? you don't say, Boston
is an actionable town they say
never been there myself
Not that I mean to slight the boys
but I've had some nice girls
from up Boston way
they turned out real spunky!
But you look like you
always did *Slinger, you*
still make me shake, I mean
why do you think I've got my hand on
my hip if not to steady *myself*
and the way I twirl this
Kansas City parasol
if not to keep the dazzle
of them spurs outa my eyes
Miss Lil! I intervened
you mustn't slap my
Gunslinger on the back
in such an off hand manner
I think the sun, the moon
and some of the stars are
kept in their tracks
by this Person's equilibrium
or at least I sense some effect
on the perigee and apogee of all
our movements in this, I can't quite say,
man's presence, the setting sun's
attention I would allude to
and the very appearance
of his neurasthenic mare
a genuine Nejdee
lathered, as you can see, with abstract fatigue

Shit, Slinger! you still got that
marvelous creature, and who is this
funny talker, you pick him up
in some sludgy seat of higher
learnin, Creeps! you always did
hang out with some curious refugees.
Anyway come up and see me
and bring your friend, anytime
if you're gonna be in town we
got an awful lot to talk about
for instance, remember that man
you was always looking for
name of Hughes?
Howard? I asked
You got it—that was
the gent's first handle
a texas dynamiter he was
back in '32
always turned my girls on a lot
when he blew In,
A *man in the house*
is worth 2 in the street
anyday, like I say this
Hughes *had a kind of interest*
about him, namely
a saddle bag full of currency
which don't hurt none
You remember there was this trick
they called her Jane—
she got religion & left the unit
but I heard this Hughes
Howard? I asked
Right, *boy*
they say he moved to Vegas
or bought Vegas *and*

           moved it.
I can't remember which.
Anyway, I remember you had
what your friend here
might call an obsession
about the man—
don't tell me you're

still looking for him
I mean they say,
can't prove it by me,
this Hughes—
Howard? I asked
Hey Slinger you better shut
that boy up!
Cut it, my friend
I was just—
Drop it!
Anyway, they say
this Howard is kinda
peculiar about bein Seen
like anywhere anytime
sort of a special type
like a lotta texans I know
plumb strange the way
they operate.

You know,
I had to deal with a texan once
nearly drove one of my best girls Out,
insisted on her playing black jack
with his stud horse
who was pretty good
held the cards with his hooves
real articulate like and could add
fastern most humans
recall before I put a stop to it
we had special furniture
hauled in from Topeka.
That horse would sit at
the table all night, terrible
on whiskey and rolled
a fair smoke
and this texan insisted he was
payin for my girl's time
and he could use it any way he
saw fit
as long as he was payin like
and I had to explain
a technical point to that Shareholder

namely, that he was payin for her ass,
which is not time!

How did you get rid of him
I asked

Well boy, that was singular
you know I thought and thought
and I was plum stumpt
that is,
until one of my Regulars of the time
who had an interest in this girl
can't recall her name
but you'd know the fella
a wrangler from wyoming, THE Word
his name was
anyway he Suggested we
turn that horse on—
Hughes? I asked.
Jesus! Slinger can't you do
something about that refugee
no! his mother was Religious
so we turned this stud on
and it took most of a Tampico
shipment to do the job
but I'll tell *you Slinger*
that horse laughed all that night
and they carried him out next morning
and put him on the stage
for Amarillo, him and the texan
sittin in there all alone
and that horse was tellin everybody
what to do
Get that strong box up there,
get them "horses" hitched up
he'd say
rollin a big tampico bomber with his hooves
his shoes had come off, you see,
and he could do it so natural anyway
and then he'd kinda lounge
inside the stage coach and
lean out the window winkin

at the girls, showing
his teeth, I can't say he was
Unattractive, something kinda
handsome about his big face
and suggestive he was
a sorta manner
he had
     He kept sayin Can You Manage?
and Thank You!
every time the hostler hitched up
another horse
and then he had a kinda what
you might call a derisive air
when he'd say "Due In On Monday"
because you see it was Sunday
when they left town, but
he kept knockin his right hoof
against the inside of the coach
sayin You All Alright Out There?
and he had the texan's hat on
a stetson XX sorta cockwise
on his head it was
I tell you Slinger you would of
split your levis and dropped your
beads to seen it.

         Because he
was sayin some of the abstractest
things you ever heard
like Celery Is Crisp!
and we ain't seen him
or that individual texan
who owned him since.
I swear
that stud must have become a congressman
or something since then
He sure was going strong on that
fresh Tampico—Some of the hands
that was there that day in fact
claimed he didn't leave on the stage
at all, there's still people
around here who'll claim that horse

flew back west when the texan
went to sleep 5 miles out of town.

Where were we I asked,
when I noticed my Gunslinger
had retired to a shady spot
cast by the town's one cottonwood
Hold on, requested the Gunslinger
and held a conference to the side
with Lil

and then he kissed with a smile
her hand and she said *you boys*
enjoy yourself, I'll see about you later.

Then as we mounted the steps
of the cabaret
The Gunslinger sang

> *Oh a girl there was in the street*
> *the day we rode into La Cruz*
> *and the name of the name of her feet*
> *was the same as the name of the street*
> *and she stood and she stared like a moose*
> *and her hair was tangled and loose . . .*

STRUM
strum
Do you know said the Gunslinger
as he held the yellow tequila up
in the waning light of the cabaret
that this liquid is the last
dwindling impulse of the sun
and then he turned and knelt
and faced that charred orb
as it rolled below the swinging doors
as if it were entering yet descending
and he said to me NO!
it is not. It is that
cruelly absolute sign my father
I am the son of the sun, we two

are always in search
of the third—who is that I asked
Hughes?
Howard?
Yes.
No.
Why not?
Because the third can never be
a texan
Never?
Yes.
Why not?
I told you, back there
when you held my horse.
Ah. If that is the case then
is your horse the Turned On
Horse of whom we've just now heard
and if that may be true how is it

your horse is also that
magnificently nervous mare
I've back there held?
Back There?
what is it you ask?

Is that your horse and was it
the Turned On Horse.
Possibly.
Possibly! what do you mean?
No, my horse is not a texan.
What?
Drink the yellow sun
of your tequila and calm
yourself, Jack
and then I shall tell you
because you are inattentive
and expect reason to Follow
as some future chain gang does
a well worn road.
Look, by the way, a fight
has started, order again
before the place is Smashed

        I then did order, yet
wondered, the inexplicability
of all that had, in this half
hour passed. And when
the divine tequilas were served
we two had retired to a table
obscure in the corner.

        Lo que pasa he breathed
this place is
in the constructive process
of ruin—Gaze upon it:
tables upended, the flak
of chips and drink surrounds us
with perfect, monday night slowmotion

        And now my Gunslinger
in his steady way deliberated
on the scene before us—Note
he said
that confusion.
I did.
What do you see
he asked.
Men fighting I answered
Is that all, he asked
Do you want the deetails
I asked
Don't be evasive he replied
What is the *principle* of what
you see.
I was hard put to understand this
I tried.
The principle, I said
is leverage. Not quite
the Gunslinger rejoined,
that is the mechanism
I asked for the principle.
Yes you did, quite plainly
said I
But I am afraid I—
Never mind he said, are these

men men.
Yes I answered on the heated margin
of that general battle
Is my horse a horse? he continued
I'm on that score not sure
I said.
Your horse seemes different
from these men.
Quite right
but that's not altogether
what I am getting at.

Here
he said, passing me the cigarette.
I think, he added
of taking you to Las Vegas.
Then you aren't going
to Boston. Not now he
exhaled, fresh distortions
as you yourself heard
have reached my ears.
Uh-huh I managed to exhale.

Thus we sat and still
I knew not the principle
of which he spoke.

STRUM

strum

Then there was an interlude
in which the brawl before our
indented eyes went on.
Auto-destruction he breathed
and I in that time was
suspended
as if in some margin of the sea
I saw the wading flanks
of horses spread in energy

What makes?
he suddenly asked in the smoke
and turmoil, and the bullets
flying,
What makes you think
oh what makes you
that this horse sitting between us
and who has not spoken
a word
or is it that I have
from the beginning
misjudged you.
The Horse grinned at me

Oh my Gunslinger, I said
If this be true
and it must be
because I can see in this horse
the Horse described
Will it not be very inappropriate
that Lil see this same Horse
in her establishment?
What of the girls?
Why, untaught alien
do you think I have arranged
this mass collision, standard in its design
you see raging not 15 feet away
but to distract the vision
of that spinning crystal?
She seemed nice enough to me
I said.
You have not lived 2000
and more years and as he
disengaged his eyes from mine
he said And speaking of said
Lady here, she, comes—

　　　My god, Slinger, she said
I am at your service,
replied the Gunslinger.
Oh knock that off!
I've got a Business to tend to

and the smoke in this corner
is blindin besides, say
haven't I met that Horse
before? The Horse
rose from his chair and
tipped his stetson XX
Hello *Lil*, it's been a long time
here have a seat,
we've got a lot to talk
about, *Slow down*
the Gunslinger said and
that was the only time
I ever heard anybody speak
obliquely to the Horse.

    Thus sat the four of us
at last a company it seemed
and the Bombed Horse took off his stetson
XX, and drew on the table
our future course.

Whispered, as I did, aside
to the Gunslinger, Who, finally,
is this gaudy Lil?   Lil,
I didn't expect to see
here—we were in Smyrna
together, now called Izmir
when they burned the place
Down, we were
Very young then
I might add. Does that
satisfy you?
Yes I answered.

    And then
the Oblique Horse
having waited patiently
for the course of that aside
to run
asked Have you finished.
It occurred to me
I might not readily

Answer a Horse
but I was discouraged,
in whatever question
I might have felt,
when the Gunslinger
on my arm put
the pressure of his leatherbound
fingers and gave me
a look
in the aftermath of those bullets
and that dispersing smoke
which said, Quietly.

STRUM,   strum

      Then sat we mid aftermath
and those unruly customers in Lil's
cabaret and the Plugged In Horse
covered the table
with his elaborate plans
and as he planned he rolled
immense bombers
from the endless Tampico
in his saddle bags.

What's happened to my black ace
the Horse inquired
scraping his chair, reaching
under the table,
smiling, passing at the same time
his bomber without limit to me.
But, I,
don't recognize
this size,
it is, beyond, me.
No, mortal, that size is beyond your conception
Smoke. Don't describe yourself.
That's right, referee, the Horse
thinks he's makin telescopes

Lil observed
but one often makes a remark
and only later sees how true it is!
Jast pass it! Hey Slinger!
Play some music.
Right, breathed the Gunslinger
and he looped toward the juke then,
in a trajectory of exquisite proportion
a half dollar which dropped home
as the .44 presented itself in the proximity
of his hand and interrogated the machine

A28, Joe Turner *Early in the Mornin'*
came out and lay on the turntable
His inquisitive .44 repeated the question
    and B13 clicked
Lightnin' Hopkins *Happy Blues for John Glenn,*
    and so on
the terse trajectories of silver then
the punctuations of his absolute .44
without even pushing his sombrero off his eyes

Gawddamit Slinger! there you go
wreckin my Wurlitzer again
sittin there
in that tipped back chair,
can't you go over to the machine
and put the money in and push
the button like a normal bein?
We're at the Very beginning of logic
around here
so them things cost money
and besides that *Slinger, some*
of these investors
is gettin edgy
since this Stoned Horse come in
they're talkin bout closin my place
Down
scarin my girls with hostyle talk.
My bartender gettin tighter
every time you do some shit

like that.
Don't bring me down Lil,
we'll be out of here by and by.

Yea Lil, drop it
the Stoned Horse said.
We'd all rather *be* there
than talk about it.
It's all right Lil, I
said. *Oh refugee*
you talk like a natural
mortal, take your hand
off my knee
I've got other things to do
now.

STRUM

Just then a Drifter carrying
a divine guitar
passed by our table and the guise
inlaid around the string cut hole
pulsated as do
stars in the ring
of a clear night
Hi!   Digger
the drifting guitarist greeted
the Bombed Horse
who was in his saddle bags
rummaging
Heidigger? I asked
the Xtian statistician
is that who you are?
Are you trying
to "describe" me, boy?
No, no, I hastened to add.
And by the way boy
if there's any addin
to do around here

I'll do it, that's my stick
comprende?
Where's my dark ace?

    Into the cord of that question
a stranger turned his brilliantined head
pulled open his fabrikoid coat
and Said
        What's your business
with Any dark ace!
            The scene
became a bas-relief
as the length of the bar froze
arms and legs, belts and buckles caught
drink stilled in mid-air
Yea! You! You're a horse
aincha? I mean you!
and, "looking around", *Horseface!*

strum

The Stoned Horse said Slowly
not looking up
from his rolling and planning
Stranger you got a *pliable lip*
you might get yourself described
if you stay on.

Come on!
Who's the horse, I mean who's
horse is that, we can't have
No Horse! in here.
It ain't proper
and I think I'm gonna
put a halter on you!

Uh uh, the Gunslinger breathed.
Anybody *know* the muthafucka
the Stoned Horse inquired

of the general air.
Hey, hear that the stranger gasped
that's even a *negra* horse!

Maybe so, maybe not
the Gunslinger inhaled
but stranger you got an Attitude
a mile long
as his chair dropped forward
all four legs on the floor
and as the disputational .44
occurred in his hand and spun there
in that warp of relativity one sees
in the backward turning spokes
of a buckboard,

        then came suddenly
to rest, the barrel utterly justified
with a line pointing
to the neighborhood of infinity.
The room froze harder.

Shit,
Slinger, Lil noticed, *You've pointed*
your .44 straight
out of town.
I keep tellin you
not to be so goddamn fancy
now that amacher's
got the drop on you!

    Not so, Lil!
the Slinger observed.
Your vulgarity is flawless
but you are the slave
of appearances—
this Stockholder will find
that his gun cannot speak
he'll find
that he has been Described

Strum

the greenhorn pulled
the trigger and his store-bought iron
coughed out some cheap powder,
and then changed its mind,
muttering about having
been up too late last night.
Its embarrassed handler
looked, one eye wandering,
into the barrel
and then reholstered it and
stood there.

strum

The total .44
recurred in the Slinger's hand
and spun there
then came home like a sharp knock
and the intruder was described—
a plain, unassorted white citizen.

You can go now,
the Turned On Horse said.
That investor'd make
a good janitor Lil observed,
if I was gonna keep this place
I'd hire him.

What does the foregoing mean?
I asked. Mean?
my Gunslinger laughed
Mean?
Questioner, you got some strange
obsessions, you want to know
what something *means* after you've
seen it, after you've *been* there
or were you *out* during

That time? No.
And you want some *reason*.
How fast are you
by the way? No local offense
asking that is there?
No.

        I like you mi nuevo amigo
for a mortal you're exceptional
How fast are you?
Oh, average fast I suppose
or maybe a little more
than average fast, I ventured.
Which means
you gotta draw.
Well, yes.
Umm, considered the Gunslinger
taking the telescope
from the Turned On Horse.

Please don't hold my shortcoming
against me oh Gunslinger
and may I enquire of you—
Enquire? he breathed
don't do *that*
Well then may I . . .
no I wouldn't do that Either
How is it then?
How can such speed be?
You make the air dark
with the beauty of your speed,
Gunslinger, the air
separates and reunites as if lightning
had cut past
leaving behind a simple experience.
How can such aching speed be.
Are you, further,
a God
or Semidiós
and therefore mortal?

        First things first

he reflected in the slit of his eyes
your attempt
is close
but let me warn you
never be close.
A mathematician from Casper Wyoming
years ago taught me That
To eliminate the draw
permits an unmatchable Speed
a syzygy which hangs tight
just back of the curtain
of the reality theater
down the street,
speed is not necessarily fast.
Bullets are not necessarily specific.
When the act is
so self contained
and so dazzling in itself
the target then
can disappear
in the heated tension
which is an area between here
and formerly
In some parts of the western world
men have mistakenly
called that phenomenology—

You mean, I encouraged
there is no difference
between appearance and—
"Reality?" he broke in
I never "mean", remember,
that's a *mortal* sin
and Difference I have no sense of.
That might be *your* sin
and additionally—
Don't *add*, that's my stick,
the Horse said smiling.
Furthermore, the Gunslinger instructed—
More is more divine
said the Immobile Horse
Furthermore, don't

attempt to burden me
with your encouragement
because
to go on to your second Question,
I am un semidiós.

And so you are mortal
after all said I
No mortal, you describe
yourself
I die, he said
which is not
the same as Mortality,
and which is why I move
between the Sun and you
the ridge is my home
and it's why you seem
constructed of questions, uh,
What's your name?

i, I answered.

That's a simple name
Is it an initial?
No it is a single.

strum

        Nevertheless,
it is dangerous to be named
and makes you mortal.
If you have a name
you can be sold
you can be told
by that name leave, or come
you become, in short
a reference, or if bad luck
is large in your future
you might become an institution
which you will then mistake

for defense. I could
now place you
in a column from which
There is No Escape
and down which The Machine
will always recognize you.
Or a bullet might be Inscribed
or I could build a maze
called a *social investigation*
and drop you in it
your name
into it—

Please! I implored him
you terrify me.
What then, I asked
is my case? looking into
the Odd toed ungulate's eyes
who had his left leg resting on my shoulder.
The mortal can be described
the Gunslinger finished,
That's all mortality is
in fact.

STRUM

Are you hungry
mortal I
the Gunslinger asked
and Yes I answered reflecting.
Well then Lil,
let's have some food
of two sorts
before we depart for Vegas.
Lil snapped
her gaudy fingers
and drink was brought
but not for the Classical Horse
who forewent drink
with a brush of his articulate hoof.

The usual he said
Usual! There's nothing
usual about your diet Claude
Lil said, *Horse chestnuts with the*
spiny covering intact
and 38 stalks of celery
in a large bowl.
Claude I enquired—
Don't enquire boy
It can be unhealthy
pass the salt
Do you get called Claude?
Why not? Listen, I,
I'm as mortal as you
born in santa fe
of a famous dike
who spelled it
with an e too.
So your name is *not*
Heidegger after all, then
what is it? I asked.
Lévi-Strauss.
Lévi-Strauss?
Do I look like his spouse!

No . . . I mean I've never
seen his wife.
You're a very observant type
Claude replied.
Well what do you do I persisted.
Don't persist.
I study the savage mind.
And what is that I asked.
That, intoned Claude leaning on my shoulder
is what you *have*
in other words, you provide
an instance
you are purely animal
sometimes purely plant
but mostly you're just a
classification, I mean it's conceivable
but so many documents

would have to be gone through
and dimensions of such *variety*
taken into account to realize what
you are, that
even if we confined ourselves
to the societies for which
the data are sufficiently full,
accurate, and comparable
among themselves
it could not be "done"
without the aid of machines.
　　　Got it! the Slinger asked
Yea, I *heard* it I said
Not the same thing he said
Tell me more I said
The Horse has an interest in business,
haven't you noticed.
Noticed? I replied
Forget it he said, remember
you're just average fast.
The Horse is a double agent—

strum

Oh? But what about his name
Claude Lévi-Strauss is that—
Yes, you guessed it
a homonym. Don't get bugged Amigo

strum

Here comes Lil.
OK, the Gunslinger breathed
we're briefed
Hughes? I asked
Not now the Slinger said
here's Lil
Slinger! that Drifter claims

he can sing you a song.
What shimmering guesswork
the Slinger smiled
and beckoned to the young guitarist.

strum

    As he travels across
the cabaret may I ask
a question? Move on he said.
Are those rounds
in the .44
of your own making?
No bullets, I rarely use
ordinary ammunition.
What then?
Straight Information.
What?
You sound like the impact of a wet syllojsm

Look, into each chamber
goes one bit of my repertoire
of pure information,
into each gesture, what
you call in your innocence
"the draw"
goes Some Dark Combination
and that
shocks
the eye-sockets of my detainers
registers what my enemies
can never quite recall.

    Another question.
Naturally.
What do you know
of Love?
Know? Nada, if I knew it
it couldn't be Love.
Even a mortal knows that.

Then, what *is* it?
IS is not the link
it takes nine hundred years
to explain one blown
spark of Love
and you don't have
that much time Amigo.
How can you?
Leave it friend
I was with Gladys,
in Egypt
witnessed messengers
turned into phantoms.

He pressed one long finger between
his eyes—
it beats me how you mortals
can think something *is*.
Hush, pues, here comes our Drifta.

STRUM

Salud, poeta
what song can you sing?
All songs but one.
A careful reply.
Then can you sing
a song of a woman
accompanied by that
your lute which this
company took to be a guitar
in their inattention.
Yes I can, but
an *Absolute* I have
here in my hand.
Ah yes, the Gunslinger exhaled
It's been a long time.

The drifting singer
put one foot on a chair

and began

I shall begin he said

the Song about a woman

On a plane of this plain
stood a dark colonnade
which cast its black shadows
in the form of a conception made
where I first saw your love
her elbows at angles

her elbows at black angles

her mouth
a disturbed tanager, and
in her hand an empty damajuana,
on her arm an emotion
on her ankle a band
a slender ampersand

her accent so superb
she spoke without saying
and within her eyes
were a variety
of sparkling moments
Her thighs were monuments
of worked flesh
turned precisely to crush
what they will enclose
and in her manner is a hush

as if she shall enrage
with desire
with new fire
those maddened to taste
from her jewelled toes
to her swelled black mound
her startled faun

which has the earthy smell
of slightly gone
wild violets

O Fucking Infinity! O sharp organic thrust!
the Gunslinger gasped
                        and his fingers
spread across the evening atmosphere
My Sun tells me we have approached
the 24th hour
Oh wake the Horse!

   Lil, will you join us
on our circuit to Vegas?
Leave this place and be done?
The stage sits at the post
its six abnormal horses driverless,
chafing their bits
their corded necks are arching
toward the journey
How far is it Claude?

                        Across
two states
of mind, saith the Horse.
But from Mesilla said I
to Las Vegas—Vegas!
the Horse corrected
have you been asleep
. . . Must be more like
a thousand miles.
More like? he laughed
as we waited
for the Slinger
on his long knees
facing the burning hoop
as it rolled under
the swinging doors west

Mortal what do you mean
asked the Horse lounging and yawning

More Like!
how can distance
be more like.

    Thus, in the thickening vibration
our departure took shape
and Lil
the singer holding her arm
followed us out the swinging doors
and into the stage coach we got
and the Horse was leaning out
making his pitch
distributing fake phone numbers
and baring his teeth and the singer
was whispering a lyric to Lil
who had her hand on the Slinger's knee
and he was looking at me

And the stage its taut doubletree
transfixed and luminous shot forth
and the Horse
pulling from his pocket
his dark glasses
put them on and spoke not
and by those five missionaries
Mesilla was utterly forgot.

Prolegomenon

to Book IIII

Goddesse, excellently bright,
thou that mak'st a day of night.
You tell us men are numberless
and that Great and Mother
were once synonymous.

« We are bleached in Sound
    as it burns by what we desire »
and we give our inwardness
in some degree to all things
but to fire we give everything.

We are drawn beneath your fieryness
which comes down to us
on the wing of Eleusian image,
and although it is truely a small heat
our cold instruments do affirm it.
So saith Denis, the polymath.

We survey the Colorado plateau.
There are no degrees of reality
in this handsome and singular mass,
or in the extravagant geometry
of its cliffs and pinnacles.

This is all water carved
the body thrust into the hydrasphere
and where the green mesas give way
to the vulcan floor, not far
from Farmington and other interferences
with the perfect night

and the glittering trail
of the silent Vía Láctea
there is a civil scar
so cosmetic, one can't see it.

A superimposition, drawn up
like the ultimate property
of the ego, an invisible claim
to a scratchy indultum
from which smoke pours forth.

But now, over the endless sagey brush
the moon makes her silvery bid
and in the cool dry air of the niht
the winde wankels across the cattle grid.

Twenty-four Love Songs

for JD

> As our eyes were held together
> we withstood there
> the space of our returning
> and passed thru a country
> of heavy, laden boughs
> from which we took nothing
> and grew thin, and strong
> along the lance of our Journey

1

It is deep going from here
from the old world to the new
from Europa home
the brilliant scrolls of the waves
                    wave
the runic secret of homeward
when Diego de Landa
the glyphic books destroyed
there were old towns
        in our hemisphere sadness
now as then

no sense in old towns chontal
                got to have
newtowns of the soul

2

Inside the late nights of last week
under the cover of our selves
you went to sleep in my arms
and last night too

you were in some alarm
of your dream
                some tableau
an assembling of signs
from your troubled day glows
and trembles, your limbs
divine with sleep
gather and extend their flesh
along mine
and this I surround, all this
I had my arms around

3

My speech is tinged
my tongue has taken
a foreigner into it
Can you understand
my uncertainties grow
and underbrush and thicket
of furious sensibility
between us and wholly
unlike the marvelously burning
bush which lies at the entrance
to your gated thighs

My dear love, when I unsheathe
a word of the wrong temper
it is to test that steel
across the plain between us

4

Or if the word falls—
    but I didn't *mean* that
too often and too soon
before it moves

carried in our mouths
into the bright orchard
of a desire we must build traps
to catch
so that we are free
we think, to answer all
who would delay us,
it is our *selves* dressed
as the clothed figures who beseech us
for Our lives to beware
destruction, *take care* is
the password to their stability

5

Carried in our mouths
the warm sperm rises
and prolongs us—as we are
everyway locked
inside the warm halls of flesh
which is in our kind
filled by a song for all lovers—
How are you? is simply
another transcendental question

I'd know you were my katalysis
had we never met, in all space
I am fixed beyond you, the cruel
is a decision of the stars, in all space
our clef is pitched together
we share
a completely trued voice
our substance carried
in our joined mouths
flows

6

The cleft in our ages
is an echoing cañon—look
I insist on my voice
Archeus become my life
and as any other extension
not to be ignored—
if you were my own time's possession
I'd tell you to *fuck off*
with such vivid penetration
you'd never stop gasping
and pleasure unflawed
would light our lives, pleasure
unrung by the secretly expected
fingers of last sunday

Do you hear me, can you
please only agree with me
because poems and love
and all that happens in the street
are blown forward
on the lightest breeze

7

But you are a green plant to me
only to be acknowledged
with passion
tended by my whole attention
there is argument only in equality
one war we can hope to ignore

What we have done is embroidered
our two figures are
as if set forth from Bayeux
and I fly like a dragon standard
yet my soul because I left home
as you did

pulls against a martingale
and having stayed at home too
or more
how much more pulls against you

8

Now the scorpion
crawls on my shoulder
and bold as the quartered arrow
of Mars though I am
beat down, too
under the drag of what
we conjure with what
choosing among the real
with the accuracy of image
we see
the problematic figure of youth
across the Atlantic
of a past love, or passed?
and there he is, reconstituted
water dressed in a freer present
than any present past
and your eyes tonight are journals
of unburnt records

9

EYE high gloria
    a fine europ ean morn ing
    black coffee
for Nick in the nick of time
he gives me something for you
and Otis Redd ing
with his feet up watching
infinity roll in and Nick
his time ing

and sudden lee the lid
comes off
        and we head straight for
the thing we could be in
cannabic warm
and rime ing

10

Who could have told me love
is always love
and all it's needs to be
where it needs to be
are you
I thought forgive me
it was something you do
now everywhere I turn
and everytime there is
that full thing with us
I am cottered
         high inside you
   lutus

11

You are not easy to enter

   Omega

you are a double letter
and I am equal only
   to my own singularity

the mixed strings of aries begins
you are sometimes in the trance of what
is beyond you,

            sometimes close
and then you turn into it
            so fast we turn

into another room we hear inside
and all the people looking
over the wall
are frozen

      12
            Not this
not that
      and not this nor
            not this or that
                  nor caught
on poles at
      all I have
                        no place
outside might welcome
might warm me

      I am nothing
anymore at all
than in myself, you be
a still center
which has about it pivoting
ramifications of my strain
a marvellously pure chrystal
the center still and in me
                        located
and in the ten thousand
years or more
            will change
      and be
      the shift, location
and polaris
      a new name

13

I feel that fear
    my own
that fear a face presents
    and looks
and says words and the words
mean something
        else
and the fear
is inside the other meaning

      meaning which

would have no meaning then
of the thing that's not itself
would fear not itself
        fear not,

could have no meaning
Don't kill me
with that other meaning

14

The largest center we know
makes his move
sundown in the window
and in space, double space
each one a concentration of
the other a difficult fact to absorb
it is a double labor to love
one twin
and Nájera crosses my table
praising the audacity of an early death
Do you know where we are now
we have come here the day after
the announcement
      and we look at our lives
      in a camera

We made the journey by train
it was cold now and then
a day scored by a cloud
the heat we had we had in our pockets
and occasionally we took some
what more can be said
more than the existence we have

15

The question is not to you, you know
the indisputability of the soul
do you know where we are now
do you know the platform any more than
I arrived at the same time one september
what was crossed
is still crossed
and the agent's dark eyes
burn from the dark short past
represent, handles the claims
of those we over ran
and they scream with their
fixed smiles
for satisfaction
do you know where we are now
from my soul I want to know
from my beginning in and out
within me
and now returned home
from somewhere abroad
on the second day of april
with the snow

16

When the duel

                    the split
the collateral
of the mirror
the sisters
in the scrolls of foam
the trans parency
of the mirror
                    in that lure
you say goodbye
you say hello
reflected, and dig this—
your personality, as such
would be complicated
even if you had been

          born all by yourself

17

The imagined
          is the quality of life Paris
not the bones in the fish
in the oppression
of La Cupole, the drama of
our time, masks, a dramatic
event dinner, turns, grin
frown, tables
a view of that world
open and filled
with the prospect, the long
perspective of the pain
of my life
in that text

18

    The Steppes
on the Plains
were the two maps
we joined, our lives
as two complex areas
a marriage
we'll never have to prove

19

My solid energy state breeds
extreme movement in juxt
aposed blocks of space

       Hermes standing

anyone from the beginning of time
will know the initiation of time
covered with sperm

20

When I heard the public story
of how they'd thrown away
their wedding rings, and how
the rings had been picked up
by the garbage men and taken
to the dump, and how laughing
finally they went out with flashlights
and found them that night I wondered
did they put them back on?

21

She will permit
any property of herself
any slanted permission
but make you know
any property is a careful
waste of time, and is
merly time

Thus it was revealed
the bed was covered by a skin
brought away from Delphi

22

The agony is beauty
that you can't have that
and sense too. There is
no sense to beauty. It offends
everyone, the more so
in ratio to the praise of it.
And I've known this for a long
time, there has been no
great necessity to say it. How
really, the world is shit
and I mean all of it

23

And then, if you come
to the mountains, what
is there more, ore in mines
ore in veins, or more fully than
you might have had it elsewhere.
Call them the Rockie mountains.
They aren't yours and

you never thought they were because
you lived in them too sometime,
someplace ago   and know better.
There is a vast smell of marriage
not lightly said, some place
some time ago I was there too.
I've been everywhere.
This afternoon I thought why not,
why not get Jenny into something
and we both fly off to meet,
well, almost anyone. Away
from the flat rancorous smell
of their insinuation, which is
just this: you've done the thing—
you've presumed your body
as well as your mind, *your mind*
we like to watch go through its sideshow
lifted up in the bright creative air
but when you made other arrangements
for your body, baby go away, that's it

24

There is no final word
for how you are.
An emotional response
can be the reputation to
which all inquiry is referred
and let go at that.

Back Home, Back Home
the day wakes up and once
out the door into what's
left of the fresh air it still
comes clear
how lovely
love is there

The Kulchural Exchange

*"Nobody loves me but my mother
And she could be jivin too"*
—b.b. king

Slinger, an idle question the poet asked
Are you considered a learned man?

Perhaps

What haps?

You meant whose

I can't choose

    I can follow that lapse
so I shall reveal to you
what I know via Information
I c'gnitioned long ago
that whatever is put in
is triggered with impurity
and however entertaining that might be
it is killing you
with the clicking routine of a rosary
therefore if there is anything to know
I shut mine eyes
on a count of three seconds
and if I get the bit thats it
and if not I have another go

What information do you have
from this process?
Practically none
just one in fact
There is a saying
they have on Mars
    "Sonne in the blue sky zero degrees
    like the first polkadot"
"Far Out,"

so you know
practically nothing

Thats correct, nothin
I'm almost
pure Exformation

Anyway, the poet urged
try a 3 second bit
and see what you get

OK the Slinger breathed
He shut his lids
and 3 seconds passed
Behind Them

What! the poet whispered

A fat man with white hair
under a blue baseball cap
and a green shirt
under babyblue bib overalls

What are his feet in?

Didn't get his feet.

You mean you didn't get the whole bit?

We rarely do, You
tell me what he had his feet in

It wasnt my bit

But Exformation is common
youve seen this outcrop
a dozen times
one place or another, dont be confused
because it comes from *My* head
Now, without trying
tell me what the bits feet were in

Uh, Shoes, the poet hesitated

The Slinger crossed his lids
to rerun the three second bit
A-minus, he whispered

Whats that for the poet enquired

     A-minus is your grade
it indicates youre slightly tired
it's like a desperately correct answer
yor imagination was fard
with a Tom Sawyer Programme
a soft con to paint the fence
Id suggest you learn to think
with a touch of sense

then you can use yor head
as an Intake for solid liquid & gas
which Must be Why
He ran a line clear down to your ass

Gee, that blows me out,
I hadnt felt it like that Master
but now I can see your process is faster
and it's quite suddenly discrete
that his feet were *in his feet*

Im proud of you,
the Slinger beamed . . .

[*Chicago Day 113*]

The Cosmology of Finding Your Place

The *Resistantism* of all other places
On the floor among filters and the Spillings
  The cosmology of the floor of the Nation
  The cosmology of finding your place
    The cosmology of smelling and feeling your Natural place
    inside the place, feeling the filters
      feeling the rock, feeling the roll
      feeling the social spray at that level
        low down, with the filters and the feet
        feeling the place you can fold all four legs
        and be man's best friend to the End, among the filters
        and the feet, in the rock, and in the roll
      in the clock and in the roll, in the hole
      of the social bilge **The Great White Dog**
    of the Rockchalk, seeks his place Seeks
      The place for Him there, tries every scrap of Space
    The Great White Dog of The Rockchalk Cafe
    moves under the Social seeking his own Place
    in the constant present snap of eternity
    listening with the german dislocated castenet
  His Nose Is under the great pin ball rolling in heaven above
  thru the barren terrain of feet He moves
from place to place seeking his place
The resisters the dogs seek their place
WAYNE KIMBALL told me all this
WAYNE KIMBALL sits in the booths, WAYNE KIMBALL
knows about the *Great White Dog of the Rockchalk*
The Great White Dog of The Rockchalk doesn't
  The Great White Dog has been there
  Western Civilization is Beer
    The Great White Dog of The Rockchalk
    went thru the door of Western Civilization
      Which is north of the Barbershop
      and north of the sailor pants incense shop
        The Great White Dog went between all that
        and the Gaslight, *The Great White Rockchalk dog*
          shakes hands with both paws indiscriminately
          For he Seeks his own true place on the floor
            He disregards the social He seeks the Place

he seeks The Space his **soul** can occupy
In His restless search he looks only for the Place
Where he can come to rest in his own true Place
and that might be on the floor of the rockchalk
The great *White Dog* is not Interdicted by opinion
He accepts the floor of the *Rock Chalk* as an Area,
like any other, he will test that space
He is preoccupied only with the Search
The Great White dog of the Rockchalk is not social
WAYNE KIMBALL told me all this, WAYNE KIMBALL
is social, he knows only persons, he doesn't
give a shit for the floor of the *Rockchalk*
WAYNE KIMBALL is neurotic like us, he wants
to smoke Grass, WAYNE KIMBALL sits in the booths
WAYNE KIMBALL drinks beer, has a part time job
pretending to be literate, WAYNE KIMBALL uses
the telephone and all other public Utilities
including Cocaine, *The Great White Dog*
of the Rock Chalk is full of shit and can't shit
until he finds his place, WAYNE KIMBALL has diarrhea
WAYNE KIMBALL hasn't got a driver's license
WAYNE KIMBALL is thin and knows everything that happens
He has ears, He is a corrupt little mongrel like us
turned on to everything hopeless and bullshit
The Great White Dog of The Rockchalk is dumb
and doesn't know anything but his instinct for the search
for his place somewhere in the litter
of the filters and the literally dropped dreams
of the *Great Rock Chalk*, he smells the dreams
on the floor dropped from between the legs
of young English majors, ejected from between the
Dual Spraycans of the fraternizers
He seeks his place on top of this matter
among the feet of the privileged nation on the floor
of the *Great shit, Rock Chalk Rock Chalk White Rock*
Chalk Dog, And WAYNE KIMBALL Smokes cigarettes
and Thoreaus them ontoOntoOntoOnto the floor
already predicated by cancer, the slow movement of *Cancer*
and I love these dogs because they are us and more us
than we are and they seek their places as do the true

whether they are *Resisters* or just scared or both
They are the twin dogs of creation in our image
and I give them both the floor as I give the *Resisters*
This Poem from the throne of Belief as the **Egyptians**
Gave and took from the Dogs Their access to Heaven
That we may all be Gods and seek our Place.

*[presented april 10, 1969, at the united campus
christian fellowship benefit reading for the
draft resisters league, Lawrence]*

The Poet Lets His Tongue Hang Down

I would Enquire of you
The Slinger leaning forward askt
One of the 4 Great Questions
Least troubling my mind since my arrival:

WHO ARE THE BARBARIANS?

    As if in a space elapsed
between our sighting then hearing a jet
The Poet grew pale
and his blazering transister fell
from his Ivory Fingers
        four of whom
        jumped off at the knuckles
        and ran off with all his rings
        and straightaway sent notes
        to the six who stayed
        expressing contempt and dismay

And the temperature fell in his veins
and his mouth weakened
and grew slack
and his eye left the track
and wandered about the landscape
unlocused and his tongue
fell out over his chin
and his nose migrated
even as Gondwana too gorged
on the immensities of time to be observed
so that its movement must be proven
by the striations of its slippage
as they are the Scars of the Earth
And his ears floated upward
as if Helium was all they heard
and his feet come off and sped over the horizon
leaving the wings of his ankles behind
        and his shoes filled with dust

an instant ghost town complete
with banging shutters and peeling posters
Announcing the stark Indifferentist proposition
       DEAD or ALIVE
when behold! the galloping Cosmographer
dropped under his mount
and blew out the OR

Then his hair fell away
in a dust bowl condition
Like in the Grapes of Wrath
and things come to that
all the people of his barren scalp
packed up and found their way to California
around the craters in this once rich terrain,
the High Planes we shall call them

And his brain snapped shut like a greasy spoon
When the last customer has et his chops
        then gone out the door wiping his chin
        with one hand While the other buys The Times
        which he reads standing on the corner
        toothpick in his mouth *Rams Clobber Lions*
        in his eye
        and turns the pages to the comics where Rex Morgan
        is performing and can't be reached
        as his hand comes up from scratching his ass
        to catch the pages in the Michigan Winde

        But the poet's Head was during this lapse
        busy with alterations
        and when the job was done
        the bang of hammers
        the whine of bandsaws gone
        And all the baffling pulled off
        his Head was a pyramid
        the minimum solid

            And his eyes came home

trying to look like the trip had been a bore
when signs to the contrary
were all over the floor

And he smiled
But the eye atop his pyramid
Would say no more

Executioner, Stay Thy Cold Blade

As knowledge grows
it becomes apparent
that the brain
is a machine
of a type
very different
from those made hitherto
by the thotfull
   efforts of man

Its success is largely due
to the richness
of its parallel circuits
and its redundancies

This makes it very difficult
to assign particular functions,
especially
by the technique of removal

The Octopus Thinks with Its Arms

Out of the total of some 500 million nerve-cells
300 million and more are in the arms

The script in the memory
does not include the recognition of oblique rectangles

In the optic lobes of an octopus
we meet the first great sections of the visual computing system
a Mass of 50 million neurons behind each eye

The optic lobes themselves can be regarded as the classifying
and encoding system and as the Seat of the Memory

The male Octopus Vulgaris fucks by putting the tip
of his third arm
inside the mantle of the female
who sits several feet away
looking like Nothings Happening for about a half hour

The females are impregnated before they are mature
the spermatophores survive until the eggs are ripe
Both animals are covered with vertical stripes during their session
and move not at all.

The History of Futures

The long horn was an automotive
package of hide & bones, a few hundred
pounds of dope which delivered itself
entirely free of moral inconvenience
known otherwise as fat
yet with a memory fresh enough to market

The Bloody Red Meat Habit
dates from about 1870
Before that we were a Sowbelly Nation
feeding off the wisest of the omnivores
Beef is the earliest element
of the crisis, a typical texas imbalance

Importations, trash beef from Argentina
are meant to satisfy
the Bloody Red Meat Habits
of our best friends, and in fact
as pet lovers secretly understand
you Can fool fido

With Foodstamps we have pure script
the agricultural subsidy farmers have enjoyed
under every name but socialismo
since World War II

Which brings us
to a truly giant dog named Ronald
the most immense friend conceivable
a Fenrir created by beef heat
and there you have your bullshit apocalypsis

One morning, in his mythological greed
He swallows the Sunne

[for my students at Kent State
Spring, 1973]

149

The Stripping of the River

The continental tree supports the margins
In return for involuntary atrophos
Which can now be called the Shale Contract
Not only are the obvious labors
In metal and grain and fuel extracted
But the spiritual genius is so apt
To be cloven from this plain of our green heart
And to migrate to the neutralized
And individualizing conditions of the coasts
That this center of our true richness
Also goes there to aberrant rest
Bought by the silver of sunrise
And the gold of sunset.

This Is the Way I Hear the Momentum

having touched the Slaughter Stone
    of the Henge of Stone
        Rock
      in the memory of
      Memory Rock

    in the memory
of Brittany Dolmen and then across
    the return into a people
      woe to them who eat too much
    from a people who eat
        too fast as
        tho it were an exercise

    yet
well being arose
    from
the emptiness
    of the stomach
  from the universe
    every change of placement
the shift of every leaf
    is a function
    of the universe which
moves outward from its composed center
      40 bilynyrs.   Then returns
               the pulse
          and location will have changed
        The location free of reference
    except this obvious measurement because you can feel
    completely a straight 5 B. years
      from some moment now which is not
      an apparent edge
    but as mappa india anna
      as the source of speech
    is no simple explosion

    our given pulse
          hits inside this
everymoment we live

                    to hear this
        COSMOS
                the soul of the universe
        calls indifferently the populations
                to proceed
                    from the tincture
                to the root of the natural
                in the present effort
                    to arise into the light
                ness of these limbs
        these parts of the universe having growth

        So the foot of this book
            is grown at last for the book to stand upon
        thrown from myself as my life was given to me
            with sharp aim
                    right across the quality/quantity question

                    When I reached the Tor
                    and walked up to
                be elevated
            enough to sense the zodiac
                of its configured presentations
                of itself the lit
                    and distant hills simply
                        the joy of expansion
                    which is what we've experienced
            for 35 billion years
            and can take in
                        the moment
        approaching when all of it
            will be stilled in a shimmy
                of its own distance
                as the thing holds so
        with the delicacy of water tension
        to avoid dispersal
            of all thats here   the wholly
            beautiful seizure of the co-
        ordinates of its distance
            the scansion of its trip
                as we come around again to feel wide open
            on the arc

Mesozoic Landscape

Anything that looks like
A Solution
is as ridiculous as the Problem

?

He read the *Coca leaves* three times
Each time they told him . .

Cascades of) **HAND JIVE**

SOCIAL CONTROL

the unit

Someone hiding all over the unit

an idea has been bouncing around
the unit in the past few hours

she let go and sprayed all over the unit

*(27 yr old athlete
admitted (to the
Unit) six mos ago
"upset because
he is getting old"*

E) eleville (mood elevators))
like a towne in Kansas

"of course this is all reviled
but then, thats the rush

And they reviled him entire
when they extracted the five o'clock shadow
in 1960 before the pepsi episode

a major invasion
of the modality

episodic lunacy

Electric treatment

an elect́ospasmodic smile graced
his lips,
as he faced the crowd
. . . lowd

mensural

ED DORN

KENT STATE ARTS FESTIVAL '74

153

RECOLLECTIONS OF GRAN APACHERÍA

First Lines

It is bright to recollect
The first law of the desert
The children of both sexes
They are of many clans
There is a season of gold
Along this spine of dragoon mountains
Tallow shampoo so the hair is sleek & obedient
When Victorio was killed accidentally
Victorios seester was no pocahontas
We call his mother Juana
Friends from boyhood
Great hardness in old age
When Geronimo was in Washington for the Inauguration
Gen. Crook proved to a skeptical world
Who can tell what a traitor is?
Captain Emmet Crawford,
When the Boundary Commission
A treacherous fiendish look   (Bartlett
This material yields
There was a time
The longest continuous run
The women circle the men in conference

The original monuments of perception
Out of the Sunset movement
So   The infant is bound
They were sentenced to observe
The train has come to rest and ceased its creaking

It is bright to recollect
that the Apaches were noble
not in themselves
so much as in their Ideas

The first law of the desert
to which animal life of every kind
pays allegiance
is Endurance & Abstinence

The children of both sexes
had perfect freedom
And were Never punished
They were wired to the desert
And they were invisible
in the mountains

They are of many clans
They usually take their names
From the natural features of Localities
Never from animals

Victorio

There is a season of gold
before the energy of a people
comes to its ritual close
and this is a metaphor not satisfied
by the mines

There is no call
to mourn the death of Victorio
he was spared the trivial meanness
of imprisonment and slavery
No principles generated
by a moral quandary in time
and in fact Apache heads
were rather amused by Oklahoma

See the pictures of Geronimos band
riding in dormant automobiles
or holding the biggest pumpkin

Yet his taste for Death
is the bitterness we find on the tongue
when we consider La Gran Apachería

He is the most dreaded
The most terrible
The most famous

Nana & Victorio

Along this spine of dragoon mountains
the pains in Nanas bit off leg
a wound inflicted by the vicious teeth
of the Alien Church, their thin line
moves north then south
across the rio bravo del norte
the winde driving the wild fire of their loyalties
and in the cruel vista
I can see the Obdurate Jewell
of all they wanted, shining
without a single facet
upon our time
and yet the radiance marks everything
as we unweave this corrupted cloth

Dress for War

Tallow shampoo so the hair is sleek & obedient
Vermilion for the face and Blue micaceous stone
    whose dust glitters weirdly
From a conejo deer an inch wide band of blood
    from ear to ear
Copperore for green stripes
The best army field glasses
    with which to sweep Hades

The most absolute of the predatory tribes
Apache policy was to extirpate
Every trace of civilization
From their province

Bounty Time

When Victorio was killed accidentally
by a breed named Mauricio in Chihuahua
the smug governor of that province
awarded the killer 3000 silver pesos
and a nickel-plated rifle which several
years later another Apache was to grab
from the hands of the bearer and blow
a close range hole in the stomach of same
this was not the importance of Victorios death

For at this point Victorios sister
assumed joint command with Nana, then 80,
of the Incorrigibles
who flew back to Tejas to clean up the landscape

The Provoking Figure of the Horsewoman

Victorios seester was no pocahontas
She must have been Something besides
the product of vicious unfair reporting
that she could split a barrel cactus
with the sharp edge of her glance
like to see whiteye throat tore out
like to smell that Mind spill over the ground
and all over Mexican ground
most of all, terrible dreams of Janos
where Mangus lay out dying and the mexican surgeon
under commission to save his life or
get the whole town burnt down
because it was old ground
where everything whiteye policy strives for
from the south: to mix himself, disappear
Tom Mix in relentless numbers over the horizon
blue endless coats turned
like everything else in the present century
to something khaki looking vaguely like shit

Geronimo

We call his mother Juana
She had him near Tulerosa
Rocket Country still
Notorious through his opposition
To Alien authority
And by Systematic
And Sensational advertising
His Pleasures were widely known
As Depredations
Among the Invader

Eyes like two bits of obsidian
With a light behind them

Juh & Geronimo

Friends from boyhood
In Chihuahua and Arizona
Perfecting their senses
In the portable forge of summer
Got down to the Mother Mountains
Their obsessive democracy
Blown out at the points of control,
Crazy with permission
A noiseless ecstasy
Only they can hear
Each man permitted
More than a man can bear
Against the true as steel
Military Republicanism
Of the Norte Americanos

Nanay

Great hardness in old age
He can be imagined
Straight from the flaking slopes

A strong face
Marked with intelligence
Courage
And good nature, but
With an understratum
Of cruelty and vindictiveness

He has received many wounds,
    muchas gracias amigos
In his countless fights
With the whites,
    muchas gracias amigos

In each ear it was his pleasure
To wear a huge gold watchchain

When Geronimo was in Washington for the Inauguration of Roosevelt he was interviewed at the Indian Hotel by S.M. Huddleson of the Dept. of Agriculture. Geronimo signaled through Geo. Wratten that he wanted to know where Huddleson lived, and was surprised and disappointed to learn that Huddleson lived in only *one* house on only *one* street. Ugh! he said in gruff disgust and signaled that if *He* were to live in the city, *He* would live in every house in it!

Fifteen Hundred Tons of Hay @ 1ᶜ per Pound

Gen. Crook proved to a skeptical world
that even the Apaches were corruptible
He put them to work in the hills
at Fort Apache
with small sickles & butcher knives

The Moving, Invisible Spectre of the Phratry on the Traitor Peaches

Who can tell what a traitor is?
To What? His own comfort?
Are there any traitors to that?
Those dying of discomfort
can accommodate it most

The brave arise
less often than the cowardly
yet the group must, somewhere
remember the mistakes
of low and common tendency
even when it is a mistake itself
when the cowardly are too remembered

What sets these things on their course?
What participle of this history
comes to have the label Decisive Moment?

It was known to be Peaches, caught out
who revealed the escape route

And when, above Janos
we asked permission of the women
to strangle the children
the women consented
and the suicide gripping
of the throats of our own children was done
and those delightful voices lay silenced
in absolute sacrifice
in the burrows where we hid
we slipped out   through the light
from Captain Garcias raging grass fire
once more to the Sierra Madre
once more past the jaws of your hungry god
the frenzy of survival rushing from our pores

A Period Portrait of Sympathy

Captain Emmet Crawford,
Commander of Apache Scouts
is sated with German Romanticism
his eyes are sunk deep
in centuries of masturbátory introspection
on his chest two ranks of buttons
and a complicated rigging of braid
he has a dark lost look
in the style of Poe
and the scouts love his weirdness

When the Boundary Commission
following Kearneys capture
of New Mexico in eighteen fortysix
arrived at Santa Rita, trouble
arose
          (because naturally the miners
          (had pushed some red hot bayonets
          (through the natives
and when they moved west
to get this line on paper
and out of the Membreño heart
into Chiricahua, they were surveying
a border long established by Apache force
And the Gadsden Purchase was made
to correct an error of omission

Assorted Compliments

A treacherous fiendish look   (Bartlett
Some have a chinese cast of countenance   (Smart
Wiederliche Physiognomien Und Gestalten   (Möllhausen
More miserable looking objects I never beheld   (Fremont
Coal black eyes   (Peters
Physically of slighter build than any Indians I have seen   (Clum
Die Lipanis haben blondes Haar, und sind schöne Leute
                                        (Müklenpfordt

Sont des beaux hommes   (Lachapelle
Geronimo is the worst Indian who ever lived   (Gen. Miles
Tall, majestic in figure; muscular   (Brantz-Mayer
Fine physical conformation   (Foote
Crian pié menor que los otros indios   (Sonora etc.
They live entirely by the chase   (Delgado
Slim, very agile, features emotionless, flat, hair not unlike bristles
                                        (Bancroft

La carne del caballo   (Velasco
They are said to be more fond of the meat of the mule
                        than that of any other animal   (Gregg

Reservations

This material yields
only insofar as the reality
was digested at the occurrence.

This material, and this
includes the famous greatness
of the B.A.E.
is the dung & piss
of Warfares invariants.

There is the Arabness
of the subject.

And it Is the supreme form
of the argument that foreign Policy
has always been an Internal policy
at the heart of the american Inability
to propagate a Central Thought.

At the base of it
One finds the Northern Europeans
marked inability
to live on Earth with other kinds
and certainly
not with kinds other than themselves.

But that this manicness
is directed like a death ray
even to their own kind
is the ultimate difference.

For instance, in our terrain,
Bandeliers wretched, derisive
reception at Fort Apache
riding on a halfass
halfhorse, or Cushing indistinguishable
among the Zuñi fruit sellers.

They are so far from home.

It now looks as if
their strategic mistake
was in not interbreeding
with the native blood
in the first days
and extensively thereafter.

Their enforcement of The
Dispersion of the slave blood
of course doesnt count, that use
is only a marriage of convenience,
derived from industrial
and technically social considerations.

And includes none of the innateness
in which the conqueror joins the conquered

Love is mistaken by Whiteye policy
throughout the hemisphere
where it is taken for necessity
and where it must contend in
a soil of distractions, always
the conqueror waiting for the spaceship
at the edge of the page
and whose biggest footnote
is an apocalypse prior to themselves.

Those who have seen in this
some higher drier destiny
of the Person
have seen it in the small alienations
of the color coded wires of the culture
but it isnt there.

In this case it is poco a poco
in the fabrications of the aer
turning back the sunlight
promoting the early return of the glacier

and it is Also possibly,
in line with our habitual craziness
absolutely nowhere.

We do not even yet
know what a crisis is.

Creation

There was a time
when nothing existed
this time was before form

Time rolled on. And space
which derives its character
from time, was not distinguished.

There now appears a spot
a thin circular disc
no larger than the hand
yellow on one side
white on the other, in mid air.

The first distinction
is naturally given.

It is to be as pure conception
not genetically argued.

Included in the disc
there is a bearded man
the size of a hand

He is the Sky Man
the agency of the metaphor
the One, who lives above.
He wakes as from a long sleep.
He rubs his face & eyes
with both hands, and where
his eyes light, light appears
Everywhere

Above and below
a sea of light.

A glance to the East
light associated with black
the South the full spectrum

the West saffron
the North blue.

The One then cast out
a ball, rolled from the sweat of the brow
and up sprung the Parentless Girl

Woman created first
out of a direct act of labor
not from some spare part
Night Girl is the nucleus of the universe.
Some other One then asked
Where is the Earth
and the One replied
to this voice of the story
I am Thinking, Thinking
Thinking, Thinking

I am Thinking Earth.

And then he thought
a Little Boy
and poco a poco
the whole phylum
was brought into being

There was great laughter
in the beginning
when all creatures could talk.

The Whole European Distinction

The longest continuous run
of external resistance:
the Apache Wars.

Without significant intermission
from the Seventeenth Century onward
can only be attributed to
the superiority of Native
over Alien Thinking.

Yet they had not invented Mind
and as we know
their domain was by Mind over-ridden

In all the treaties
the Native assented
                       to the Thinking

And never, and
have not yet discovered
the predictive Mind.

Personum

The women circle the men in conference
they speak like a loud annotation
to every advance of Thought

They are theologically overheard
Those who overhear them
log each nuance of the record

A clinic attention to the future
is not to their nature, they ask more
Of the immediate utterance

They have no mechanic of the future
And
They are prepared to meet the animate

If now they lie dormant

They were by Mind overcome,
I have a mind
is the highest mutation of force

The original monuments of perception
are the play of light
through the wall's membrane

Out of the Sunset movement
Out of the Sunrise invasion

So   The infant is bound
    hand & foot
    to the cradle board
    a platform with roof
    balcony onto the World
    shield to the sunnelance

    They began life in this manner
    devoted to pure observation
    from head to nock
    And of course without
    the petty distraction of their fingers
    waving pathologically at the future

    Because, it is from witness,
    they made no natural cause
    to fear the future
    Their art was
    of cosmic physical proportion
    the scale proposed for everything
    and reflected in their landform

                    Their leading ideas
                    come directly from the landform

        By the time they are let out
    they have seen it first
    from the frantic jog of escape
    to the just plausible image
    of the desert floor
    and what is before them
    invites them to get ready

The Slipping of the Wheel

They were sentenced to observe
the destruction of their World
The revolutionary implications
are interesting

They embody a state
which our still encircled world
looks toward from the past

Gen. Miles imagined
That Geronimo
Didn't know
The function of the heliograph

La Máquina a Houston

The train has come to rest and ceased its creaking
We hear the heavy breathing of the máquina
A relic in its own time
Like all the manifestations of technical art
And without real gender
And hidden from direct appeal
By the particulates of the English language
Itself the agent of frag mentation
And lonely accuser of the generic lines
The heavy breathing of the lonely máquina
Stopped in its tracks waiting for the photograph.

The Apache are prodded out into the light
Remember, there are still dark places then
Even in the solar monopoly of Arizona and Tejas

We are with the man with the camera
They step off the train and wait among the weeds
They never take their eyes off of us, wise practice
We motioned the way with our shotguns
They are almost incredibly beautiful
We are struck and thrilled
With the completeness of their smell
To them we are weird while to us
They are not weird, to them we are undeniable
And they stop only before that, they are like us
Yet we are not like them
Since we dont recognize that. We say:
One cannot have a piece of what is indivisible
Is natural Apache policy
Where for us, that is a philosophical implication
We are alike, but we see things
From behind dis-simular costumes,
The first principle of warfare
Where *All of Us* is the Army, and they are the people

Precisely they step off the train
And this is an important terminal moment
In the Rush Hour begun in this hemisphere

This is the moment before the leg irons
They look Good. They look better than we do.
They will look better than we look forever
We will never really look very good
We are too far gone on thought, and its rejections
The two actions of a Noos
Natches sits alone in the center
Because he is the elegant one among them
Hereditary, proper as a dealer
He is inherent and most summary of themselves
Supple, graceful, flexible hands
Goodnatured, fond of women

As the train moves off at the first turn of the wheel
With its cargo of florida bound exiles
Most all of whom had been put bodily
Into the coaches, their 3000 dogs,
Who had followed them like a grand party
To the railhead at Holbrook
                              began to cry
When they saw the smoking creature resonate
With their masters,
And as the máquina acquired speed they howled and moaned
A frightening noise from their great mass
And some of them followed the cars
For forty miles
Before they fell away in exhaustion

HELLO, LA JOLLA

Shifting an Interference with Nature to a Scientific Obstruction

Humming birds are close to junkies anyway
All that keeps them straight is the flower
And her control of plenitude in their cause
Curbing their overweening gluttony
And their insatiable singlemindedness
Yes, as the books say, they are pugnacious
But in them it is a quality absolutely without wit.

So when this normality is disturbed
And they go for sugar in water and acid red #27[a]
They do get vicious as the supply gets low.
At this point Harmonics drive these hovercrafters
Crazier still, as it punctuates their slavery[b]
And their birdbrained anger spreads
Throughout their frenzied holding patterns
Sugar, sugar.

---

[a] Index number for the notorious red #2.
[b] An experiment conducted at 110 degrees Farenheit scale (a mere 70 degrees below the fundamental interval) by Jeremy Prynne, using the upper registers of a #365 Marine Band Hohner.

Wet Cake

Did you ever get the impression
standing in the supermercado
that an awful lot of people,
in California, want the *water*
but they'd just as soon skip the rain?

What Will Be Historically Durable

About Nixon[a] there was
Something grandiose
Although this peevish society
Failed to even blink at it.

Nothing illustrates this
More than
When he stole the post office.

---

[a] Yet, it is too easy to use one whose very name is a satire upon all government. (taken from Junius)

An Opinion on a Matter of Public Safety

Air Bag sounds like eminent sickness
This device should not be permitted
General Motors was right to suppress it
and wrong to have relented
and Nader should stay out of it.

Driving is based on alertness
whether that be loose or tight
Those who let their attention wander
must not be encouraged to survive
by a bag full of air.[a]

---

[a] Airbags are a good example of Say's Law, which says that production creates, notoriously, the product, but the market also. And of course, the rationale, in this instance, Immortality.

You're Supposed to Move Your Head,
Not Your Eyes

We now live next to the tennis court
Yellow green balls seem to be the thing
this season. For phrases we get
Vicious shot! Or, I *knew*
you were gonna do that!

Last Saturday we watched
the finals, inside. Vilas has got
an arm like a gorilla, and
it appears, it also serves
as his main instrument of thought
since it returns the ball
so often to the same place.[a]

Outside, on our court,
the less consecutive thocks and thucks
labor along on raw audible time
dramatized by the brain's impatience
with bleak, netted balls.

Connors' paranoid study of his strings
reminds the nation that tennis
is the only game in which the instrument
suffers the blame for error.[b]

---

[a] A tennis intelligence is subtle up to but not including the shot.

[b] Even the Dentist, that meanest class of sportsman, when he breaks your tooth, doesn't exclaim Shit! as he critically stares at his pliers. Footbol, both types, is perhaps least dialated by this instrumental paranoia. The passer does not glare in hatred at the hand which overthrew the pass, nor does the kicker inflict punishment on the foot that missed the goal. The hunter does not throw away the gun that missed the duck &c.

ALASKA: in Two Parts[a]

From the rear window of the Lockheed
we begin to pick out the Islands
of the green black archipelago
while inside the wingéd cocoon
a wild laughter issues from those
who go forth for the first time
cheered on by those who return again
to the expectation of this inflated emptiness.

This might feel like a certain moment
from the history of land grabs.
Another sublime promise
from a faithless future.
But the mode of transportation
changes everything except the mentality.
The desperation of walking
beside the household luggage
is lacking here, this is rather
a laughter of fraught nerves
not the undifferentiated search for space
we've always served.[b]
This is starting from the shacks of Burkburnett
not from the salons of Kansas City.
The biggest single overcast
the longest white line
on the green tundra, the maginot
of this occulted place, like
a bumpersticker too famous to repeat.[c]
And the largest single cabbage
whose image is distributed on a post card
but as symbols, vegetables are dumb.

---

[a] For A. H., of Sitka.

[b] There are two main kinds of cruelty: That which is enthusiastic, and that which is un-
necessary. The period in which we live practises the latter.

[c] The curious can ask around. I never once saw it on an actual bumper during several
weeks of observation. There is a corrupted version of it in a photograph of a desk motto
(sign) in N. Geog. #5, 150.

Across the gridline from The Voyager
stalwart stands the Captain Kook
"trusty" blondes in adamant short skirts
50¢ coffee, passable in extremis
1$ egg, a tradition from the Rush.
The food tastes like it was just
shipped in from Mars.[d]

Two men of equal height
appearing in pioneer beards
carry a vinyl couch[e] downtown.
Idling taxi outside window
speaks to a moose far out in the bush
night falls, more gradual than slowmotion,[f]
this place is sultry
like a sunday school class.

The stories are thin and complicated[g]
destinations restricted.[h]
Brand new cars, hoodsprung, rimsprung.
Telephone dial tone an insect's buzz
an echo of the summer evening.
And then one day one wakes up sharp
with a great lump of ones in one's poke
a residue left over from the evaporation
of volatile fifty dollar bills.

---

[d] The domestics are said to eat wild meat from freezer coffins.

[e] CH_2CH, a hydride derivative of ethylene, probably from Texas, probably from Gulf & Western, sure to cause cancer of the butt.

[f] The length and utility of summer day is notorious in latitudes near the Circle where the season becomes a diurnal extrusion and the sunne takes on the powerglides of a big Sandoz pill, and the population gets a little open-eyed rest in the brief crack of twilight. "The sky is full of parhelions of delusive glory."

[g] Or ursine and certain, as an arm torn from its socket. The bears treat this place like muggers do Manhattan.

[h] Big denomination dope and L.A. women might be the exceptions.

II

We would have somewhat more interest
in reincarnation if there were
less insistence on mechanical joints
in the transmissions,
but it is perhaps too touched
to dream of a return as a glacier
where that is a deeply turquoise dream,
a resonance of outside time.

Here we witness
the rumble of constant adjustment
here the earth moves, not
from the keenness of our perception
but from orogeny, its natural employment.

The blocking out and stringing
of the continent's shoulder
where the river is the mainline
and the island chain a broken arm
bent awry from the body.
A few natives will learn
to be its undertakers
among the horde of hikingboots[i]

Will this be, as it is publicised,
the last great land adventure?
Generally that's meant real estate.
We're not working with an exception
but for those who want the real thing
they're going to get it out of a can
or disappointment will rap their knuckles.
Trucking is not an adventure.
It's a service.

The creatures of ice feignt and advance
with a consciousness a great deal more
pervasive than the rise and fall of wages.

---

[i] Athletic and asthetic appreciation is invariably destructive. the force of nature is never
considered destructive because its ends are unknown.

The tremendous pitch of their crystal stacks
the vast smell of their lunar coldness
the mammoth draft of their freezing humidity
the highminded groan of their polar turns.

From a beer-ad point of view
the fauna are impressive, evolved
to crush jeeps with a single swat,
and that's well enough, while socially
Alaska acts as the pardoner for every
haywire merchant with a will to get there.
But the power we behold is in the blue ice
and the delicate flora of the permenantum.
The people whose tradition it is
to live there will do best to carry on
picking up the threads of snow
from a system which is the book on survival.
That work will not be read
by all the cancritous Tej-okies
nor by the national geographic natives
in their copters & sanscrits.

The Burr Quote

Law is anything which is
Boldly asserted
And plausibly maintained

The Sociology of Games

In soccer
when you do something good
you get a hug and a kiss

In american football
when you do something good
you get a slap on the ass.

A Variation on Vallejo's #III

The layers are stilled by water
The waterhens are killed
And the entire general world fills
The night of the earth
Resting between glaciers, blocks,
Joints, the shoulder of the system
The stillness in the ice,
The grand specimens trapped there.

We are the children of weather maps
Our only book is a canyon
In twelve volumes, a work
Widely available in a shorter version.

Palms, Victory, Triumph, Excellence

My L.A. began in 1947
when I was in high school
and the derricks were still up.
I was fresh from Illinois
enlightened by Malinowski.

The excitment was not
in The Light, even then
beginning to be obscured
but in the Palm Trees
those companions
of the dinosaurs.

They are as snobbish as ethiopians
in their attitude toward man.
They follow him everywhere
except where it gets uncomfortable.

My favorite palms are in Riverside,
ol'downtown.
When someone told me
they are the preferred dwelling
of rats
I was emphatic in my disbelief
and in my disapproval of the possibility.

But of course, rats are smart.

A Discovery

The extremest pleasure
(is) to step on the Devil's neck,
and yet to enjoy the use of him

29 September

Public Notice

Don't use my name
Unless you love me
But if you do & you don't
Send me some money

Whereas

Poetry is now mostly government product
the work of our non-existent critics
is unnecessary, the grades assigned
to meat will do nicely:
> Prime
> choice
> good
> commercial
> utility
> canners

(Listen, if anybody out there's)

Listen, if anybody out there's
saying, you know, there's
something new, and something
else or other's not, well,
they should look it up.

A Mild Threat

I'm going to put you in a petri dish
and there I'm going to grow you
not all of you, though, for instance
I'm not going to grow your head
and I'm not going to grow your body

The Whiner, Obnoxious as ever, at latest report

The child was even weirder
than the progenitors,
Loud, Spitting,
Rude and Offensive
with multiple and brittle defenses.
No wonder they caved into
his every devious whim.
They knew, because he was their offspring,
he was the test of their very worst aspects
and that non-compliance
would be a repudiation
of their very own worst selves
and so they supported a social menace
in order to hide their own, inner catastrophe.

Success?

I never had to worry about success
Coming from where I come from
You were a success the minute you left town

Alaska Revisited

I would have a lot more interest
in reincarnation if there were
less insistence on meat in the transmutations
But perhaps it is too ambitious
to dream of one's return as a glacier

Not so bad after all

The keynote speaker,
A Theologian from Somewhere
Explained that "one"
Could have pleasure
And God too.

CAPTAIN JACK'S CHAPS/OR, HOUSTON MLA

Deplaning, & getting learnt

> "Some supervenient cause of discord
> may overpower this original amity."

Shaving lotion fresh
we nonstop into Houston:
Hughestown, the tool company,
the Cobra Bit, the bit
that bites the Springhill Formation,
Sugar Sand to the trade
wherein lie the cretaceous corpses
back of traffic jams.

Dobro lost some instruments
somewhere between Denver
and the ground under his feet.
A lot of bystanders, craning
their necks, had "Serves Him Right"
in their dodgy eyes, high twitch profile
all round Houston International
said to be *the most thieve-ridden*
airport in the universe.

What did he lose? A delicate Plains Harp
and a joke piece which was best lost.
When aimless personnel assured him
All was Gone,
Dick merely stood with his arms full of cases
his mouth going nowhere like an excercycle,
manifest blinking, and probably
an intense thirst for sugar
pervaded his jaspered personeity.
    Of all the hits, sugar levees
odious reality the most. That's crust.
Everybody likes a good crust,
and from this we deduce the super-ficial
should be *more, not less*, in abundance.
And it's a very good substitute
for confidence.

So at this point Dobro
unwrapped a kilo of halva
from under his montana hat
and had a good chew,
and out of the yellow door
of the cab he hailed
poured the sugary beat of calypso
when Down-Town-Hughes-Town
he drawled
with a ludicrously sour curl
on his mouth.

             *   *

At the Cowboy Panel

> "I have no sympathy for poets."
>
> Max Apple

About an hour before lunch,
a little late,
we entered the curtain walled chamber.
This crowd numbers about two-hundred,
western specializers of various breeds.
Several genre novelists decant
the vintages of When *I*
Was Growing Up in Houston,
and: The Change Has Been Radical.
As if a blind horse couldn't see
the forum of Pennzoil Skyscrapers
among the weedy trees in their holes
all sprouted 5 minutes ago
in the ash of real-estate riots.

The Word, more succinctly put here,
was *Cowboys is done*, prepare yourself
for the Oil Novel, of which there are
only a few, hand fed, examples. At least
let us pray it isn't The Novel of Oil:
in this game,
Squeeze an Arab and Houston Shrieks.

The panelists were at a table
along the wall, slightly elevated,
I mean, by a platform.
For every Larry McMurtry
there's several thousand babblers,
Max Apple being just one of them
spewing gratuities all the way
to the Pecos.

Ricardo's nerves are not designed
to take such bargeloads of tedium.
And I was too tired to laugh out loud.
Lapsed into a coma, his tic rate dropped
precipitously to an uninterrupted

horizontal line. It made me
as anxious as a TV doctor.
His neurotransmitters
had gone to McDonalds.
This was a one-man epidemic
of Encephalitis Lethargica!
The limbic system under severe strain,
I had to get him outa there, even
across the street, to the Sheraton
for, our hopes dashed, we would have
a quick orange juice instead
of the horror and agony we had counted on.

      *   *

Sunday Morning in the Murdered Territories

This poor, old shoetrod
piece of paper
blowing in the Houston breeze.
Trash trying
to individuate on Main Street,
in full view of a population
of bright-eyed & nude manikins,
their privacy protected only slightly
by dingy storefront glass.

Scrumptious meals, it says,
prepared completely from scratch.
But who wants to eat scratch?

    We've just come from Don Wesling's
room in the provocative Hotel Lamar.
A lively party with the La Jolla bunch.
Dobro played the banjo
and laid out the stunning propaganda
of a life of abandon to several candidates

who had spent an elongated day
interviewing for jobs the size of
needles in haystacks, and in the end
taking what solace they could
in tales of the motile.

Maximum Ostentation

Hyattecture is all strut and stage
and a cheap high to move through.
The inner space is hollowed-out egyptian
and although the Egyptians
were not squeemish about slave labor
their engineers wouldn't have created
a structural episode like Kansas City.

In this franchise,
the most worn-out lobbyist
drinks from the cup of absurdity
because there is Forever
one more drop of it in the cup.
A dollar bill glued to the floor
will arrest half the parade.
From that clue I take it
Dobro Dick is somewhere around
grinning through the foliage,
inside the cocktail well,
a copy of *Hobo* in his chaps.

A distant background audio
of blowing out of pipes and flues
spreads like gas
through the Titan scale of the lobby.
Dizzying verticalities of glass
launch themselves as from Cape Canaveral.

Single, sharper sounds penetrate
the gas, as if just arrived
from galaxies found only in The Catalogue.

Through this half-tone crescendo
debauch the footpassengers
from the Sheraton to the quartzy elevators
visible as ants bound for the Van Allen Belts,
only to return in the grip
of their ionized bagatellas
raincoats & umbrellas
shock smeared across their kissers.

Out comes the book.
The crowd stares at the bill
stuck to the floor.
Dick promises to levitate the money
and with it the floor
of the surrounding dynastic structure.
The grins tighten around the mouths
the fingers around the briefcase handles.
This audience is educated.
Dobro's theatrically darting eyes
set the moment
when the bill rockets into his flat hand
with the stinging snap of the rubber band.

Outrageously gag-shop stupifaction
sweeps across the onlookers
followed by beach devouring
waves of disgust
as over the face of the fakir
wash oceans of smugness.

The reading from the book
itself, is a barking affair
with the index finger, right hand,
poking every fifth word
like a jack-hammer on epilepsy.
Hungry as a lexikon, no mercy,
no thinking, no rest.

Round and round the cocktail well
the ambulatory reading draws to a close.
I've read the story, but catch
my favorite line: "I'll cook you
on a stick, before I let you
join my gang." The curtain
comes down on late afternoon.
The intellectually imperative
Gerald Graff vacates the premises
and swims through the tide of Yellow Cabs.

Our boomlens now swings upward
to the lofty balcony of the Chicago Suite
and its peculiar allurements.

    Dark suits, almost abstract pinstripes,
and no doubt the highest percentage
of eyeglasses in the dynastic structure.
Things are not *that* romantic around here
although the Green Knight himself
would likely be welcome,
if he checked his axe.
Nothing is weird here. Not even
Captain Jack's Chaps, showing
the history of all the crawling bugs
in Idaho. The Dean actually agrees
to store the instruments in his bedroom.
Drakonian tolerance. Peanuts and Allusion,
brie and Reference, and UCLA women.

      ·   ·

Hotel Hartley
Down by the Bayou,
As Dick prepares for New York
And I turn my thoughts homeward.

Secure, with the rumble of Wig-Town
in the background
Secure from the rumble of breakfast
and dinner and Miss Lily
the Big Band Chinese Songbird
who could have sung for Less Blown.
Porcelain beauty, swathed in chiffon
a fresh mandate from each wave of MLAers
seeking exotic space in Sheraton outbacks.
Shut at last from miniscule administrators
and lugubrious speculation
on sweet and sour knucklebones
and the ham of harangue,
processors to be sure to eliminate themselves
though to hear them tell it
it will be everybody else.

    Standing on the balcony
overlooking Main Street
I can hear Dialin' Dick on the line
to perpetual Lost & Founds. As one can infer
a certain degree of conversation
from the evidence of the nearest conversant
his strenuous descriptions of lost instruments
reflect a disbelief in mandolinguitaraphones
on the other end of the line.

Across the Bayou the massive warehouse
which is the "campus" of University
of Houston Downtown (we never saw
the Gilleys Department) where Mr.
Goodwrench is President,
the windows are awash in the evening light.
The traffic splashes in the fine rain
cut, once in a while, by a pedestrian
hunched against Hughestown's loaded Dice.

High tides of preoccupation . . .
it might be entertaining
to chase some mice around New York
as regards the invitation,
but then, thinking of the labor of travel,
it might not.

There is the almost audible crash
of nugation from Morktown
and the memory of the bitter mountaineers
surviving in their lofty Hel.
And I think of Tom Clark far to the West
at the bottom of the Pacific Rim
and whose post card I have in my pocket.
Bicycle grease smeared on his impatient face,
his hair matted with chain oil
his eyes locked like tracta beams
on the slack little SoCalers
and the bane of their immorality.

The only keeper between us
and Mr. Sarcophagous.
The Inventor of the Eighties,
the first man to copyright a decade.
The formulator of the great, post
Einsteinian equation of radical non-entity,

$$ESH = MASS$$

And Dialin' Dick dials on,
again to New York and Montana,
a conference call of stuttering sublimity.
My brain is like jelly,
all I need is some toast to go with it.
Tomorrow morning I'm going home.
If I don't cast myself away
I've got a fair chance of getting there.

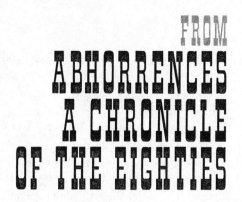

FROM
ABHORRENCES
A CHRONICLE
OF THE EIGHTIES

■

one bullet
is worth
a thousand bulletins

The Protestant View:

that eternal dissent
and the ravages of
faction are preferable
to the voluntary
servitude of blind
obedience.

While You're at it

As long as you're closing The Window of Vulnerability
would you mind shutting that door of paranoia
And while you're at it, would you mind
sweeping the carpet of disdain.
And then there's the container of trash to carry out
When you're finished with that
you might go to the kitchen where you'll find
the skillet of rashness. Uh,
just throw in a few slices of the bacon of compatibility
and fry well.

January 1983

Wait Till the Christians
Hear About This!

In his effort to get prayer into the schools
President Reagan reminded us
that the ancient Romans and Greeks fell
when they abandoned their gods:
students needn't "pray" exactly,
for instance, they might "think"
for a while before school starts.

If he means that, Thought could get
the biggest boost it's had for years.
Maybe they could think about some greek myths.
And what about sacrifices?
I wouldn't mind seeing Cap Weinberger on a spit.
Maybe they could consider the Aztecs—
I wouldn't mind at all
seeing Jeanne Kirkpatrick's frosty heart
raised to the heathen skies.

Flatland

People make a lot of fun
of the Flat Earthers,
but the fact is,
in a lot of places
the earth is flat.

December 22, '83

> "On the Interstate," with
> R. "Dobro" D. Paycheck strip,
> south of South Pass. Shortbeds,
> longbeds, hotbeds, waterbeds,
> close shavers, coupon savers.
> "The only good martyr's
> a dead one . . ."
>
> Raymond Obermayr

Rough Passage on I-80

We are travelling through the country
where "Thank you Oh Lord
for the deal I'm about to receive"
is chiselled into the blacktop
like a crow's incantation.

It's minus 3 degrees
on the Count Fahrenheit scale.
It would be Boraxo country
except there ain't no Boraxo.
And no mule teams. Here the mules drive.

Those rolling hills out there
are full of coal and oel and moly
a lota moly, that's lybdenum

the kind of denum the cowboys
around here wear. Around here everybody's
a cowboy with no cows
and every cow is without boys.
The boys have all gone to Rock Springs
to drill and to get shot.

    Low trailers hunkered in the Winde,
the big snau-blower. Scrap rock, like deinosaur fins
strung along the saurian freeway. Ah,
to endeavor to gain what another endeavors
to gain at the same time—competition!
eight barrelled, sharp clawed!

    The graft is longbed style, Shot the Sheriff
fur shure, plus some shot the D.A. types,
they're all here. Tractor hat Stranglers,
Drive-up Drinkers, Mobile Snorters,
Pass on the Right Siders—mega rednek,
and for good reason—they've lynched all the Lavender Neks.
More dangerous than Beirut.
They don't take hostages,
they don't take anything alive.

    White rock faces, Four-Wheelers,
Big Dealers, Slim Jim Peelers,
Teased Hair Squealers! YaaHoo!
beller the Yahoos, it's where
they make the springs rock—
they don't call it Rock Springs for nothin'.

RADIO: White Christmas scrap,
Der Bingle baritone in motheaten night-cap.
We see through the landscape:
black rubbermaid crows
sail past a turquoise trailer, cold aluminum
hunched under the guns of the winde.
Inside the sleeping resident turns
on a couch of budweiser cans
lips frozen turquoise, wrenched,
limbs on the pike to gangrene.

RADIO MUSAK: Gordon Lightleg!
dulcimerland, vests on pennywhistles,
Folkak, Blusak, Rucksak Rock.

On to Rollins and Riggins.
Steel mosquitoes probe an oel poule.
Deinosaur blood, black and crude,
the awful, devious oleo-olfactory
death odour, atomic weight 32, low and volatile,
driven by the pistons of hell,
the transfusion of the red roadmap,
where those stumping bags of the autoperiod
were once given to roam. Out the window
the Prontosauris Oil Company
sits next to the Horny-toed Boot Factory,
Overthrust Belt getting looser and looser now
after the gas these "Big Boys with popcorn teeth"
sucked out of the mantle.

On the asphalt cinch, rolling along,
kidneybelts tightened, the Kenworth Tractorsaurus
stampede into Wamsutter, Lusk, Dittlebone
and other such turquoise-eye-shadow towns.

The Wamsutter Hotel is totally electric.
Gas, permanent vacancy,
Conoco, Amoco, nowhere to go.
That Big Trailer over there
is where the Mayor lives,
pole light on all night,
prowling dogs, cringe and slobber
for an ankle to crush—not the friend of Everyman.
All this would be on a hill but there ain't none.

Gay Johnson installations
on both sides of the Strip.
The Howard Johnson of the High West.
A woman built like a stack of tires
fills up her coupé—SIGN
"Gay Johnsons, Buses Invited, Tobacco."
On second thought, Howard Johnson

doesn't deserve
to be the Gay Johnson of Wyoming.

   Roadkill scattered like throwrugs
on blacktop. All the groundrunners
are either smart (located elsewhere)
or dead at the wheels of the heavy hitters.

Speedy schools of pickup trucks
scatter ahead of hunter packs of tractorsaurus,
Terribledactyl birds,
ghosts of old clavichord players
swoop with heavy grecian wings
to snatch up flat rabbit fleeces
from the altar of the tar, Wyoming crêpes
dredged in pea-gravel crude.

RADIO: Governor of Wyoming Safety Bulletin:
Recommends strapping skis bottomup
on roof-rack in case of flip-over.
Woman held in tract house by unidentified
Gillette Krak Dealer—across town six onlookers
killed when police check out false report
and man rains lead on the unpaved avenue.

   State Trooper ahead between the strips,
coffee thermos in officer's fist.
His police shield doubles as Rad Badge of Courage.
Snow fences, like arthritic twigs of protozoa
vanish into the vale of snow—the world is getting colder
as the transmitted propaganda says it is getting warmer.

TRANSMISSION FROM GILLETTE: The Razor City.
Serious roadkill this time—they're digging with backhoes
and throwing the victims in.
Gillette: people have been known
to go there just to have their throats cut.
AD: "Trucker's Mistress,"
a truckstop item hooked to cigarette lighter
with concertina wire stretching to vitals
for over-the-road Mechanical Head—

available in truckstop gift shops
with Chain Wallets and Turquoise Buckles—
"A *real herpie saver.*"

    Laramie exits flash by like marked cards.
University of Wyo. What do they teachem there?
Nothin' works with ranchin' anyhay these days.
There they go, canterin' to the subcafeteria
in search of teflon heffers. Say!
What do you do when a Wyoming Cowboy
throws you a pin? Run like Hell!
because the grenade in his mouth
is about to go off!

    Willie's on again . . .
all the truckertops and lesser heavy hitters
singing along under parts-shop, feedstore web hats,
the houseflies washed out in the strenuous amphetewake.
"On the Rode Again. . . ."
Three Hundred pound Choir Boys
with eyes like strawberry-coconut donuts.

Crawling to Little America in Cheyenne.
Twenty-six degrees below Count Fahrenheit.
The transmission from Gillette fallen silent.
Cut off by the authorities no doubt. Somebody asks
how interesting can a town afford to be?
The soft, reasonable talk of Denver
supplants the airwaves, the jittery compromise of the city
crowds out the spontaneous stix.

    A yellow ivory ball of pollution
hangs above Cheyenne's fibreglass air.
The Santa Claus-bright Gettysaurus Reks Refinery
is strewn along our approach, blowing
not so symbolic mushrooms, MX Missile Burgers,
the biggest meat in Strip Town.

Martyrs are a dime a dozen around here.
The best ones have been dead a long time.

Recette Economique

15 September 1984

I've always found much
to recommend
in the slogan "Soak the Rich"
but I've never found
much discussion regarding
the uses of that marinade.
I have one modest proposal:
feed them to the poor.

Armalite Resolution

September, 1984

I'm not going to be
a martyr to politeness anymore.

When I see someone with a slight cold
it's the other direction for me.

Self Criticism

October 1984
Americano Style

I accept the present emperium
for my own, individual good.
I have been striving to become miserly
in all I think and do so that I,
and those few who look to me
for their protection, shall not
be alienated through my recalcitrance.

And I will not be tempted to consider avariciousness wretched,
I shall not wince or shudder
at happy talk, for even as I know it is vapid
and inane, still it is better that its users
be spared the dark tribulations
which might otherwise occupy their consciences
and distract them from their self-righteousness.
And I promise not to consider self-righteousness
in the old, aloof and superior way
which was formerly my wont.

I know that abortion is wrong
and should be shunned
and I shall banish from my mind
the scenes of infanticide
which are condoned the world over
for the good of subject states.
But those questions, again,
I will make myself reluctant to contemplate.

I will approve of genocide in Central America
because it is proprietary
and conforms with our government's policy.
I approve of the reluctant delivery of food
to Ethiopia's starving millions
because that country has a Marxist government
and I agree that magnanimity
in such a situation would be mistaken.
But above all, I am in agreement
with all my government does
because to think otherwise
would be to make of myself an enemy of the state.

When concertina wire is strung along my street
I shall not object, nor will it disturb me
because I am now convinced
that what I formerly took to be
a restriction of my spirit
is in reality, for my salvation,
if salvation is in my future,
but even that doubt is a sign of my humility.

November 12, 1984

It Could be Anyone

It is total nonsense
that if it looks like a duck
walks like a duck,
talks like a duck
swims like a duck
fucks like a duck
it is a duck.
It could be the guy next door.

#

ABHORRENCES

November 10, 1984

*There's only one natural death,
and even that's Bedcide*

For the Post-mortem amusement of Richard Brautigan

Death by over-seasoning: *Herbicide*
Death by annoyance: *Pesticide*
Death by suffocation: *Carbon monoxide*
Death by burning: *Firecide*
Death by falling: *Cliffcide*
Death by hiking: *Trailcide*
Death by camping: *Campcide*
Death by drowning: *Rivercide*
                        Lakecide
                        Oceancide
Death from puking: *Curbcide*
Death from boredom: *Hearthcide*
Death at the hands of the medical profession: *Dockcide*
Death from an overnight stay: *Inncide*
Death by surprise: *Backcide*
Death by blow to the head: *Upcide*
Death from delirious voting: *Rightcide*
Death from hounding: *Leftcide*
Death through war: *Theircide & Ourcide*
Death by penalty: *Offcide*
Death following a decision: *Decide*

*drawing by
Tom Clark*

Ed Dorn

200 copies printed April '86 at Bloody Twin Press
with financial aid from the Ohio Arts Council

The Price is Right: A Torture Wheel of Fortune

The show did not start off
auspiciously, the contestants
were nervous and kept fiddling
with the wires attached
to their privates, the men
being especially anxious
over the question of balls.
The women were more querulous.

The first question, a medical subject,
was why had the anti-abortionists
not mentioned, let alone commented on,
the Baboon Heart transplant?
One terrified contestant guessed
it was because the moral majority's
nervous concern with evolution
precluded their bringing it up.
That hopeful contestant's face
reflected the malicious light
in the eyes of the host who
immediately *threw the switch.*

A powerful surge shot through
the wires and both sexes screamed
and writhed, to the delight of
the vast viewership, estimated
at 100 million, all of whom,
presumably, were delighted
not to be on the show,
because not one in a million
knew the answer.

Another Springtime in the Rockies

April, 1985

(for P.M.

I called up to see
If I could make a citizen's
Arrest on the telephone—
There were about a thousand people
I wanted to arrest that day.
The answer was No Dice.

Then I called up to see if
I could get arrested on the telephone
For demonstrating against
The C.I.A. because I didn't
have time to go down
to get printed & mugged.
The answer was No Way.

How's that for freedom
And what does it say about
Our highly touted & deregulated
Communications system?

December, 1985
From Denison

I like a Busy View

Framed in the french doors
shut tight against
the anti-therms
evaporate the cuttlebone snows.
Along the barrel of Broadway
rifle compact cars
the next-to-the-next-to-the-last dashboard,

new master of destiny—
the program that
stands in for the tube
during the commute.

Across that perilous divide
the Greeks in their big tatty houses
hold endless tupperware orgies
with soft punk junk.
Quivering over it all, the Great
up-tilted permian slabs
who measure Travel Time in aeons
who consider carbon mono
just a passing gas, and ozone holes
letting the sunshine in.

February, 1986

Lackey stacked upon lackey

The one red leaf, the last of its clan
sails across the crusted snow.
The afternoon is mild, water fallen weeks ago
runs in sparks under the new sun.
There's nothing to do with Valentine's day
but observe a moment of screaming
for all the love that was of no account
and all the misleading feeling.

An Exception for Courtroom Behavior

In Sparks, Nevada
people should be allowed
to show up drunk.

I'm Clean, how about you?

I never ordered a general
   into Central America
   although there are those who did.

I never dumped any dioxin
   at Times Beach, although
   somebody must have.

I never made any money in Lebanon,
   although I guess some people musta done.

I never put engine oil in salad dressing
   but you know it happens
   all the time in Algeria.

I never shot anybody,
   but people do it all the time
   and as far as I'm concerned,
   they're shooting the wrong people.

I've saved a few lives in my time
   just by dispensing some good advice,
   but that doesn't count
   and anyway, it's the wrong direction
   because this world cries for death
   and practically nothing else.

In that respect, I've missed
   all the big events:
I never fed any lions in the Roman Arena
I never massacred any Protestants in France
I never gassed any Jews
I never owned any Slaves
I never scalped any Indians
I never spread syphilis in Tahiti
I never macheted any joggers.

In fact, I'm an exemplary non-entity.

1 May, 1986

Harvesting Organs: **On the Head-Injury Death**
of a 24 Year Old Boy in Vermont

Several Specialists "flew" in from Pittsburgh.
Please pardon the anthropomorphism there.
I don't mean to suggest raptors—
they're just carrion birds.

Whereupon they tore the fucker apart,
called him Skin & Bones.
They freezedried his butt,
chilled his skin. Somebody else
is wearing it now—who *is* wearing it now?
Probably some lawyer in Topeka.
Or maybe a wag in Wichita.
The fat from his posterior
now fills out an anorexic gal in Scranton.

The heart went to Houston as usual.
There is sense in this—
Houston needs all the heart it can get.
The boy's eyes went to Denver
a place as plain as the nose on your face
in dire need of vision.

And what did Pittsburgh get?
The most perishable goods, the liver
and maybe the spleen—
whichever, you can bet Pittsburgh can use it.
Look at its history, think of its past—
it has always been a big consumer of organs.

All the other parts, right down
to the toes, all the way out to the branch banks
to someone in need of a new set of knuckles,
the boy's parts were scattered through
the vast black market of the medical abattoir,
thrifty now as the Hormel slaughterhouses
of Austin Minnesota. Yet very few, if any,
of the "recipients" would be black.

    Note: the very first attempts to put
    the hearts of baboons in the human breast
    occurred in South Africa—the surgical anxiety
    to find a primate substitute
    for the scandal of the obvious.

Ah well, even as we repose here
studying the ramifications
of this cryogenic express,
they're out there, under the flashy lights,
gleaning the fallen fruit, the strange fruit—
and this time it's the bourgeoisie who are gathered.
After all, they run around the most,
they are the fittest.

4 July, 1986

Ode on the Facelifting of the "statue" of Liberty

America is inconceivable without drugs
and always has been. One of the first acts
was to dump the tea. The drug that furnished

the mansions of Virginia was tobacco,
a drug now in much disrepute.
Sassafras, a cure-all, is what they came for
and they dealt it by the bale altho it
was only a diaphoretic to make you perspire—
people were so simple in those days.
The Civil War saw the isolation of morphine
making amputation a pleasure and making
the block of wood between the teeth,
which was no drug, obsolete. Morphinism
was soon widespread among doctors *and* patients.
At this date interns, the reports tell us,
are among the premier drug ab/users
of said moralistic nation. "Rock" stars
(who notoriously "have" doctors)
consume drugs by the metric ton
even as they urge teenagers to Say No.
The undercurrent of American history
has been the running aches and pains
of the worn path to the door of the apothecary
to fetch cannabis and cocaine elixirs
by the gallon. It has been all prone
all seeking Florida, Ponce de León
was just the beginning of a statistical curve
whose only satisfaction would be total vertigo.
His eager search for youth has become our
frantic tilt with death and boredom,
in fact we are farming death in Florida
with far greater profit than we are
farming food in Iowa—elixirs are as multiform
as the life-style frauds we implore,
a cultural patchwork fit for a fool
in the only country in the world
with a shop called the Drug Store.

America the Buick

A smouldering red light—
in front of me a Buick
with only the U I remaining
on its cracked white paint job.
The roof lining hangs
with tattered effrontery
and could harbor bats.
Coils of patched flex
bounce and twist in the backseat
like hollow pythons who have adapted
to a diet of carbon monoxide.

It all creeps off then
to yet another useless, low-scandal,
shady, local destination.
It's not a compact, it's not a mid-size.
It's stretched alright,
but the work
wasn't done in a body shop.

A time to buy and a time to cry

These are the official symptoms
of cocaine use:
weight loss, insomnia,
nausea, anxiety,
radical alcohol
and tobacco intake,
chronic irritation,
helpless involuntary verbalism,
possibly leading
to fulminant dementia—

Wait a minute!
except for weight loss,
those are just the pathologies
of an afternoon
spent at the shopping mall.

30 August 1987
a little aria

Martyrs Opera

It's all way behind California here—
not much satanism to speak of,
the big sacrifices are to Impatience
and the sufferance of the routinely insufferable:
a too long queque into Full Metal Jaquette,
too few Xtians with too small bullhorns
at the opening of the celluloid
temptation of the Lord
almost reconverts the neo-nonsmokers.
But they don't need it—the smoke
still smoulders in their overcooked brains,
and melts the aloe on their malevolent lips.

Gaudy, laminated portraits of themselves
hang from their necks
not the image of some fearsome mullah,
not even close—they have so little neck
and no stiff devotion. When they break
their coffee grinders
they blow off their retarded dogs
with lawn darts assembled in Ciudad Juarez,
and do not think twice.
But that's good—the fact that
they think once is the horror of it.

the hazards of a later era:
variation on a theme

I would like to thank you
for the plums that were
in the ice-box, but
I'm afraid I just can't
do it—in the first place
it's not an ice-box, and the plums
having come from California
are a mix of over-ripe
and hard-as-rocks,
both undesirable states,
no doubt shot through
with systemic chemicals.
Add to all that
the fact that I put
them there myself
and you have
the whole sorry picture.

Recollections of Advice to Whiteguys

Be observant of people around you;
Anyone could be a terrorist.

Avoid piles of luggage or unattended bags.
If you hear gunfire,
Which sounds like catspit,
Or an explosion, fall flat on the ground
But remember, if you do this involuntarily,
You're already dead and everything
you see is just a re-run.

Never sit near windows
or any kind of glass, never go near glass.
Always sit with your back to windows,
Things have changed a lot
Since Bill Hickok's day.

Never let a bellhop take your bags,
Do anything, a karate chop, a sharp
kick in the groin—but even better,
Never have any bags. And never
Attend unscheduled meetings,
But to any meeting always take along
An armed witness.

Be observant, but don't overreact.
In most cases you will be ignored
Or worse, charged. If you have bad feelings
About anyone around you, leave immediately
But not with alarm—don't look back
Let your witness do that.

Especially be wary of "friendly locals,"
the original terrorists. Look around,
Evaluate. Who is weak, who, in biting,
Has swallowed the bullet?
Nervous wrecks should definitely be avoided.

Finally, avoid heated discussions.
Don't panic. Be cooperative.
Never make gratuitous sudden movements.
Eschew stickers like "Up the Army" or
"I Love New York." Hit the Deck. Leave Quickly.
Above all, don't be proud—
In the event of fire you may have
To crawl through heavy smoke.

Progress: slow but inexorable

He set out to buy the American Dream.
First, he went to a yard sale
and bought himself a yard.
Then, he went to a garage sale
and bought a garage.
Next, he went to a porch sale
and bought a big porch.
Now all he needed was a swing
and a house and a car.

In the smoke of
the "Western" media glee
over the spilt blood
laced with a little ap-
prehension for reduced
business. 7 June, 1989

Free Market Chinoiserie

There will never be enough BMWs
for the stated Billion, there will never
even be enough paper towel
or gas barbecues or ever enough ribs
or sauce for those short ribs. There will never
be enough coupons to clip or scissors
to clip them with—and there will never be
enough accountants to count it all
or paper to keep the accounts on
or discs to store the accounts
for which there will never be entries enough.
Someone should tell them.

The End

Did you know that
when they execute you in China
they send your next of kin
a bill for 1 Yang (28¢)
to cover the cost of the bullet?
This is the very definition
of frugal management.
Maybe Bush can learn something
from Deng after all, maybe
there's a pow-wow under the kow-tow.

It's a good thing Reagan
didn't know about this practise.
He'd have considered it tax relief.

El Peru/Cheyenne Milkplane

PROLÄG

Th' acetylene sun hung over the Ocean of Oceans
Flooding the quick afternoon of El Peru,
Casting the World shade on the gasaer jungle of Amazonas
Putting to bed the gene meat of the protein chains
Fueling the epidemia of cheap labor,
Cooking the slummy stews of cholera, cooling
The constrictors with its withdraw', slowly deepening
The tone of the washed out neon, mocking
The fitful tungsten strung along in the shadows where
The Luminosa don their Chinese hardware.

Across the tierra helada the temperature
Plummets and cracks, beyond the altiplano
And the Eastern Cordillera and the Plains
The stranglers take another hitch, and the Lianas
One last jack and hoist as they reach for the fleeing light.
Everything trends toward gigantism, giant spiders
[Theraphosidæ] "the bird eaters,"
Roam the forest gloom, centipedes a metre long

Who feed on native children drop from the canopy
Onto the sanguinolent commerce of the jungle floor.
Dynastes beatles the size of a fist, Water Boa
With the girths of court eunuchs haunt the galleries.
Butterflies, like the spectacular blue morphos
With a span of 50 centimetres, whose flash
Can be seen from more than a kilometre away
Send errant heliographs in the twilight shade
While within it swim fishes too terrible to class.
   The Nazca Plate subducts this neozoic mess
Scorching the continental basement with frictional stress
As out of this tectonic scene magmatic froth
Erupts with showers of 'candescent trash
And the expulsion mixing with an assault of basalt
Spoils the thin wake of the El Peru/Cheyenne flight,
And the passengers crowd the windows of our craft
To ponder and growl and hail this mighty sight.

ABOARD THE TAN AM
WITH ODIN, A DOG OF JUDGEMENT

   ODIN is a dog of wealth and fortuna
in a world where "its a dog's life"
is as often a human fate as not.
He was heir to seventeen million held in trust
through an uncontested settlement from his owner,
a kindly and traditional old villager
who still drove her great grandma's electric car
to market.
   Odin always felt embarrassment mixed
with the pride natural to dogs when they ride
whenever she took him out in the antique machine,
with her blacklace glove on the tiller—
for she was a sweetie and he was a killer.
   And lo, during the heyday of the Gipper
the Seventeen Great Units had increased
with the criminal returns of the times
and left him loose, with the means to keep
his noes in the air for the slightest shift
in the millieu any new tunes from the venue.
It was pleasing him now to be on the Cheyenne flight
to the rendezvous, he certainly reckoned,

with Yo Ochenta, Over the Road Pal & Paladin,
Phaëthon of the Haul,
known to most as simply ¡Joe!

   It pleased him not so well,
we know that from a slight twitch of his docked tail,
to be reading a film review by Pauline Kael
in the *New Yorker*, a somewhat predictable slick
he saw from time to time in el Peru,
But when he came across her assertion
"a bit of gonzo demagoguery that made me
feel cheap for laughing," Odin looked out the porthole
at the Ocean of all Oceans and El Niño
brewing some turbulence for the future,
grand houses launched on the Malamud,
an assembly of images awash in avarice.

   He retracted his tongue
and breathed quickly through his back lips
to dispel the Evil.
   He knew some Big Dogs along that coast.
Some had Human drivers; usually Irish—
Philipino grooms and oficianadas
to sexus canus, who moaned, and cried out in public
and who paid for every thing they wanted
in gold and dismissed their critics with "¡Here!
a Thousand Rubles—¡Go Home!" thrown
with desdän into the street—a tango of contempt.
   He opens his mouth and his tongue
lays out, a little off the side of his mouth—
the pressure and dehydration intense in the cabin,
the tortured meso-american spine curved below,
the smoke of fresh volcanos smouldering
from the rupturing subduction of the plate.
   Dogs were not meant to fly, he muttered,
picking out the updated homonids from the Dogs . . . .
   If this was in the hairy days—five hundred thou B.C.,
their bags would be cooler than they are. I am
very happy not to be sharing their bloodtype.
   Our race has known them
since they could walk on the ground
—and carry a stick, ¡¡what magic!,

what impromptu rule, what easy acquiescence
to a minor threat, the invention of attention
the future police wand, the First Rule . . .
Aye, in those times they roasted us on that stick
when their inflated ambitions
made them sacrifice the entourage,
the pack of dogs and the family of slaves.

      From carrion for scavengers
to scavengers proper
—it comes from hanging one's tongue out
but it takes more patience than magots.
How they lost that hair no dog knows.
But there are races that haven't entirely—
      His attention reverts
to the review under scrutiny:
this #'s from the Time/Rom—pre-
Fujimori—what an airbus! he muttered.
El Niño deploys grenages, updating the system . . .
. . . He recoiled his tongue and swallowed
      Having once toured the autotowns
he knew Mr. Moore's documovie from Saginaw
electric bus, lunchbucketopolis
one false move and you join the depression.
Grim, raw Michigan-town reality—a strictly
business-empire approach to class—let'um freeze
don't throw'em a blanket, *they didn't pay the rent.*
Da! Haul'em off¡!

Pauline Kael should be exiled to Flint
for that remark, he curred in a velvety undertone,
or have a homeobox patch applied to her mouth.

Did I hear you say A Homeo Box
patch¿
      An ivory white female Saluki,
legs long and fine, well muscled thighs,
bred for blistering turns of speed
looked up across the aisle—What box is that?
shaken the long silky—feathered hair
close hanging down her pertinent face.

Odin smiled and tipped his impressive head.
and looked across the Pacific,
his tongue in midMouth—
That is one soignée Gazelle Hound, he mused . . .
that platinum mink stole is not from the tropiks . . .
I said "I should have filed
instead of clawed"—Simply a mental note,
delivered aloud, in the style of my late mistress
a diary of her reflections for my improvement
That's a human trait the world over,
the desert beauty agreed, but rare in dogs she thought,
flashing her hazel oval eyes—
would you like to curl up over here? she suggested
sweeping her long silky tail around her skimpy skirt.

Odin studied the breed:
Saluki from Saluq, an antient town
of Arabia . . . way back North African & Asiatic line
tall slender swift-footed keen-eyed hunters
having long narrow skull long silky ears straight forelegs
strong widely set hind legs, a long well-feathered tail
and a smooth silky coat ranging over white to cream
black or black & tan, Umm—this one's pure cream.

So Slughi, you wanta buckle down or not.
What I'd like to do I'm apt to put off—and that's
good advice for die whole Welt.
Besides, I like the prospect from here,
and the space through which we converse be fixed,
so unless we crash, we'll never part
until we reach that sticksy Wyo aerodrome
which for now doth be our common destiny

Whereupon he sailed a card over the bobbing head
of a slobbering Biped child staggering in the aisle—

```
CAVE CANEM
picket fence perpetual security
"We only bite what's wrong"
Specialties in Internecine War
Valkyries for rent
O.Odin, Prop—J'ai Beacoup du
Chien
Crosslink 4-15-7-8-9-10
```

The percipient hound caught the card
in her feathered paw, and scanning the text
asked the winner of the Iron Cross
What more happened in Peru
under Llosa and Fujimori?
    Well, the Working Dog began,
checking his Bulova Automatic,
sticking his tongue out and yawning:
The Pizarro brothers landed—kicked a little butt,
toppled some Idols, melted down some effigy &,
outlawed the chewing of leaf, brought it back again
promptly when production dropped, Hey!
cut off some head, requisitioned some treaz—

    Stop That! la chienne deli softly curred, I mean
die Explosion before you enplaned &
the nature of your 'enterprise' in Lima—
if we can call it that, and why is a fine,
"High Tona" dog such as yourself
travelling on the suborbital?
I'm talking about the ruckus in Caracas, about
the commotion in Cali, was that your entourage
or what? Were you accompanied or chased?

    A little of both—in my business
it amounts to the same thing.
But to reply to your question:
I operated an academy in Lima
until Very Very recently (he glanced
at his Bulova)
and actually my school is wherever I happen to be

instructen die Businessmen to think like terrorists—
it comes totally natural to them.
That's not surprising, given their inherent proclivities.
Business is a form of terror—you leave the victim,
the customer, even the mere low-end shopper wasted,
drained of cash and will and shackled to the future—
wage-slaves of les Rentiers.
  The difference is you don't kill'em,
you just pillage the village—
it's a licensed operation. When all has been stripped
but the desire to go on, then you finance their revival
at rates collectable only by goons wearing hats
and driving automobiles with whitewall tires
in crude and ostentatious former times
but now enforced with a few ugly stabs at the keyboard.
It's called "Das Neubizznes." It runs on Cheap Labor
and this time it's gonna stick.

  Oh cher, how chilling, shivered the sensitive Saluki—
How do you do it?

There are two approaches to private security.
The Givem the Keys to the Benzi and Hope for the Best School,
also known as Throw Money at Its Feet and Hope It Stumbles.
(ie, playing on Biped susceptibilities, you understand) . . . .

A patch of rough air brought on the seat-belt sign,
and the artificial Tan Am voice
pointing out the eternally obvious.
Miss Saluki fusses with the hardware—Je deteste
zees abominable biped arrangements!—and clicks it shut
across the long curvature of her flank.
  Odin gazes out the window at a Banana Republic
brightly lit by the tropical sun with some volcanoes
scattered about, poking thru the mist, and mutters
No, we Do have some bananas. Und das's das Problem.

. . . . And the other school is My School,
real paleomodern,
hard edged defense, with a lota plate implied.
Violence werks, that's why your enemies use it liberally.
Sendero (to take the immediately receding hegemoniacs)

comes on with at least a bundle of dynamite, Minimum—
they're Very post-korrekt.
      I school my clients in throwing it back
and before it hits they've got das Werthers outa their belt.
When the homocorps
walk out of my sandbagged academy
they've danced around
and jumped over live ammo, they've spun a car
and hit the ground:
when they leave home thenceforth they'll be packing
die Kanone, loaded & loose.
It's the New Bizz, and It is Booming—
Terrorism is Business & Business is terror:
      A mercury switch could tilt even now in the hold
where our undelivered cagéd bretheren are shivering
and whimpering in their K-Mart Porta-Pets
and we *know* those Kennel Ration Barkomaniacs
in transit from one Retroapartment to another
are right now howling their mindless brains out:
or an engine could separate from the wing—bye bye
mama I'm off to yokahama—criminal mechanic,
neglecting to run the fatigue check, criminal executive,
ordering a speedup. Look Out Sioux City,
Look out Keokuk! Some got license, some don't.
Have a nice day, or *Carpe Diem* as the latin dogs say.
      One of my clients, indeed one of my Products,
is the redoubtable (Very doubtable I should say)
Stanley South—practically started a gusano farm of his own,
used to take an airforce jet down to the Isthmus
around tee-time just to load up with Pineapple.
He was strickly into rough terrain
but nobody could lay a finger on 'im—then
Bingo! he founded Cocaland,
the monumental theme-park obeisance
to la puissance de la drogue outa Tingo Maria,
a jerkwater cocabush town in the North.
      Whatimmer, for South, it was ein Come-back.
What a produktion—picture a jungle fort in der neuwest,
Peruvian cops in U.S. fatigues,
led by a Scwartzkopf Simulacrum in Green Issue,
they run in to U.S. kopters and chop chop

off to the other end of the runway
where Cocaland is awake and busy in the bright morning.
    Smiling, chewing, singing peasants drying leaves
they've, Ha Ha, harvested—across the way men in sombreros
do low-end chemistry on the leaves to make paste—
in front of a hut two "Colombianos" wearing gold power-chains
drink booze while a jungle box blares Salsa y Chicha.
    Now the drugkoppers are landen and sweepen.
We hear the ostentatious piñoneo of their Israeli firearms.
Small groups of combatants establish a safe distance
and after making eye contact, khoreograph their punches.
The Sombreros immediately confess. The touristas
walk along with l'armée and lumpennarcos to a shed
where presto a plump sack of cocaine paste is waiten
—Colonel South has the nerve to charge admission
to this wooden performance.
His philosophy is that it doesn't *take* a whole minute
to reproduce a sucker—that gap-toothed sonabishi
was definitely into der Schlupfwinkel heimlich big time,
runnen gunnen und hitten die bedeckung!

    Hé, lighten up on das Deutsch, d'accord?

    Kein Problem, Odin curred. I must say,
among my 'ped students, he's the least trammelled.
Setting him among his own kind is against their ethics
as it ought to be, but they do it all the time.

    Odin lifted his lime and soda
To the Millennium of the Dogge, it is way long overdue!
. . . Of course **none** of that is on my card.

    Saluki shook her silky ears, *Of Course!*—
I hear you curren.
See that Dalmatian in the first row?
His spots overlap—no good for show.
Mais, c'est la question-clef:
why would the homokorps
hire a *canine* (she said the word
with a certain elevation of her Showtime nose)
to instruct them in such arts against their own kind—

even granting your dangerous aura, dating
from the Roman invasions et cetera? And
in possession of 17 million Americano, what's the point,
even if you are a Working Dog.
        Also, and it may be none of my businesskonzerne,
but the 'ped writing this must be the biggest nutcase
in modern poetry to lead with a Rottweiler.
It makes me nervös.
By the way,
are you on vacation?
or is the Academy "on the market?"
        Odin straightened his Iron Cross, cleared his growl
and smoothed out his tee-shirt which read *Ou est Peltier?*

        Well, it's only a convention, isn't it—given the right
transgenics, I mean, a dog's as good as anybody, sometimes betta—
You don't look like *you're* taken de hintertreppen!
But whatever the case, you take the Epic you can get.
Any move to the *merely* heroic, brave men fighting
to get home or to avenge their kinsmen
aims at a solemnity higher than its original.
No feast in the Hall
no schwartzen Wölfe grabben die Hündin! [and by the way
did you imponder that testimony from the Kapitol
about the judge who allegedly showed pictures
of DOGS FUCKING—true or not, that was truly disgusting
from my point of view.] It really hit die Sturmglocke!

        En effet! I was shocked and humiliated even to hear it.
I would never Think of showing *them* in such an act,
the indignant beauty concurred.

        Natürlich, Odin agreed, we have no equivalent.
The sheer writing of the poem must be our shelter.
And the use of slightly unfamiliar words and constructions,
along with the distant knell of archaisms, all
the relentless manipulation to supply big time æther
overarched with magnanimous austerity.
These poor devises alone must now do
what the whole occasion did for 'omer. So
lay off the hack, he labors "bei Nacht
und Nebel" as the sated populi toss and snore.

And as for the inheritance,
a lawyer smarter than any dog gedroppt a lot of it in Miami—
but it has had a Texas recovery—plenty
enough to go into das Business.

Da Si, shook Saluki, smoothing her feathering, "On the 'orses!
Whereupon they both barked as if in quotes
and gave each other a High Paw.

Several Bipeds turned their heads
and squeezed their Newsweeks in discomfort.
"Jesus—transgenic dogs," one of them muttered,
"why didn't they take the Airbus!"

Odin ran his tongue over his impressive teeth
and observed: from the minute that species
stood up and walked the planet was doomed.

But seriously, we all know now
what the man meant when he said
"You ain't seen nothin' yet!"—
it's when the genome come home to roost:
Protein Chaingangs dressed up to look like scientists
in white coats and droopy socks and dumb hair.
More crooks in banks than in the prison system.
My biggest customers are bankers,
so when it came time to clear out I taught the last class
the entry that closes die Books,
the one we rarely get to teach, and Shot Them All.

Just Like That?

Essentially.

Even in El Peru
there are some rules, I do believe.

¡Sin Duda! Rules for the fools.
But in das Businessenvironment
there are no rules (that's the point: mustn't drive
away die investing Klasses), plus
mass murder is not to be found in the Book of Crimes.

It is found only by the impromptu tribunals
who try the Werkingklasses. Shooting the clients
before "turning out the lights" is considered practically œcological
if not merciful in the die Garantie.
There's nothing more Secure than Death.
  ¡Verdad!

War may be an art,
but Security ist eine Technikalscienceschaft—
    In any case, don't forget that Business is terror
and since terror was my business I just left a note
taken credit for el Sendero, and,
after spraygunnen several of their slogans about
[Chinga de Madre de Fujimori, among them)
I punched in the code to set the charges—
a not very baffled sequence ending in **delete**—
then shot der Chauffeur who was holding the door,
    On the way to the Aerodrome I phone ahead
saying I was eskapen an attack and would need
uninhibited entry and total cover, otherwise
"the lust of fiction would be punished by the contempt of truth"
or something like that—it's more impressive in Quechua.
The Timing moreover was as close to parfait
as a mere computer can get: you noticed when I entered
that as our eyebraus raised together,
there arrived the waves of some vast explósion!

    Vraiment! Saluki curred, the pulsation entered
when you did and no doubt both 'peds and quads
were plenty tired of le waiting—
but I must admit I thought "What a dog!"
and I thought. "Quel sang!" & "Oh, how korrekt!"—
big shock waves *really* turn me on!

    Now the hostess saunters by
asking what's going on with Y'all Quads?
    We were just laughing at the Mosquito Coast
down there on our right Saluki offered, We were wondering,
in the spirit of Das Businessenvironment,
what the Gringos are going to call it after the papers are signed.
    The hostess stared out the starbord hole—
good question, she thought—

I don't know, she said at last, But I'll bet it's not Mosquito.
No Way Odin chimed in. Mosqujito bad for developen—
der kamakatzi Syringen can spread Anything—
anything you can get and Everything You Don't Want.
Those pilots are the Levellers.
They just take it from where ever.
It's the most random sample going.
They have surpassed the Domini, "The Dogs of God"
in their blank indifference.
The Hostess studied the Rottweiler.
Mental note: one cold dog.
"Not surprising," she said—
but some folks are not going to like the sound of that.
By the way Miss, if it isn't too forward,
what's that patch behind your ear for?
Saluki started, and appeared nervös—Oh, that!
she whispered, is a Trans-Derm-Scop Disc—
I've been deep-sea fishing.
The Air Hostess looked into the desert creature's
liquid eyes and saw a yacht heaving in the swells
over the Peru Trench . . . .
So, the hostess blinked, what'll you
Deux chien have this time—it's "on the plane."

Well Done, grinned the Rottweiler,
I'll have a Ripped Mass
with a splash of testosterone!
The hostess turned to la chienne de chasse in expectation—
The same with a little tincture,
the canine beauty said,
shaking her feathery ears, but hold the testosterone.

Just then the tocsinless signal of the planelink
drew Saluki's attention. She picked it up—Bueno!
It was a salesman. How did you get this number? she asked.
A marionette filament of voice came through the uplink—
I looked in the Phonebook.
You Read Too Much! Saluki curred, as the silky hair
rose on the back of her graceful neck.
You sound like a mongrel. So what have you got?
Mig-29s. They're cheap and they're hot—also
I can get nuklear for between 300 to 1200 a kilo americano—

and concerning die Epidemie have you thought
about investing in Rubber Goods? Are you
interested in a space station? Slightly damaged
needs body work, some panel replacement
        No, I'm, not! Saluki was offended now.
(due sans doubt to the space station
and its association with experimental Dogs)
I'll take a Mig though.
Just put it down off I80 at the Sinclair airport.
load it with Microbombs; Tell'em it's a Zero.
I'll *Take an IDIQ* the evening of the 6th of December.
I'm booked for take-off at a quarter-of-an-hour before dawn
Send the bill to Big Saudi—and Get Off My Link!
Some Dogs!! The desert creature could barely suppress
her grinning indignation.

        Odin glanced up from his reading material.
He was now amusing himself with *People* Magazine,
a subject, at least, in which he had a professional interest.
He incurred that The Mongrel was just dumping inventory.
The gunrunner's night never ends—
it stretches out to take in the day,
its blue eyes never fade. Gunrunnen is the final morality,
purchasing power stripped to the bone—if that species
was put here for any other reason, nobody's mentioned it.

Saluki noted the Panama Canal.
Actually he's my *chef d'équipement*—everything
fabricated of detection-defying polymers. He's a whizz.
His motto is "Stealth is Not Enough." If you can kurb
your compulsion to be haughty, he might give you his card.

        Well so far that's an If-and-a-Half. Is that dogge
transgenic, a single-gene mutt or what?
I think you've got yourself a biped traveler, Odin.
Looks like you've been penetrated.

        Watch your language!—you can catch diseases
just from the way you talk,
why do you think even Perfect Celibates die?

Vraiment. But there are no celibates among dogs,
I take it you're alluding to the troubles
consuming the homo-saps.
Tout de même, this mongrel seems quite studied.
He lets his tongue hang out like a regular mutt,
no pretense of any kind to modulate his wild nature,
as one would expect of an authentic
modern member of the genus canis.

And that K-Mart jacket he's wearing—
is that supposed to be some kind of punch-line?
Let's face it, if that's the dog I just spoke to
he's still doin' it in the street *dans le rue*—
Somebody forgot to shut the door on his Pet-taxi!

You obviously move in refined circles, Odin discurred.
Der Mischling's Businessenvironment is pocked with Plastique.
Why bother with a smart jacket? The limits of tolerance
are reached pronto. There's no useful profile in that fevered arena—
these runners have no claim on truth or diligence—
they've got High Speed and Nitroglycerina.

Whoa, Odin! Saluki encurred,
Hardware and Nitro really do it to me, it's the Stuff
of which I can't get enough, it's the opposite of bananas.

Richtig, Odin incurred
Can you tell me the name of that town down there?
sparkling in the thin equatorial fog
Fifteen hundred metres above the deep blue sea.
Settled by Basques and converted Spanish Jews,
Notorious now for its evil patrimony from The Traffic
which has become the base exchange of half the World
having a value ten times that of ingot gold—
and, to be fair to the better side of town,
there is a statue of Carlos Gardel, the greatest tango singer
who ever lived, always accompanied
by fresh flowers and the salutes of the multitude . . .
he crashed here, on the approach to what
became his last and final date.

Oh Please have pity! The first thing I did
when I went transgenic was to learn the Tango—it had been
the only one of their accomplishments I Yearned to duplicate,
The Only Thing—*Tango-milonga*,
the long measured human walk,
the compelling instrumental finality of the steps,
the orchestral sweep of the social symbolization,
the dreaded vocalizations of the *tango-romanza*
and the *tango-canción*. When Carlos Gardel bought the farm
in Medellin, that bleak night in 1935,
the son of the arrabales died,
and the dreams of the porteño began.

Saluki was having a closer look at the valley sprawling.
Hourra! she excurred, there's a mess of dogs down there
and they appear very restless and hungry.

Too many dogs the lower Odin acurred.
When you were run by the Mohammedans,
were you aware that the most scurrilous epithet they have
for the European is "a dog?"

You don't understand the laws of the tent, Rotweiller.
In their world, dogs of high breed are part of zee seraglio.

That's repellent, Ødin offered.

En vérité, that's why they do it, Saluki recurred.

Across the Cold Hiss of the Nightflight
Odin Enters the Downlink

The Bipeds snooze and snuggle in their pillows,
their slowly firing idling brains,
their somnambulant systems
halting and hunting like an engine,
along their dampered hertzian waves,
A cargo of nuisances transiting l'Amerique Centrale—
"Das big Konzerne" has got a CLOSED sign
hangen an der door

The lights are low . . . the cockpitdoor is open
the digits of red and green glow like embers
throughout das Sústem . . .
on the ground the deathsquaders buckle
their Israeli hardware and prepare to lock & roll

The Rockies hold a good crop of snow
this spring Odin learns from the Storm Link—
the toilet bowls and broad green lawns of Denver
will be eager to receive their share of the drip,
as they will, if Phoenix don't suck it down first.

Vachement! Saluki raised her glass to toast.
Vraiment, vous avez du chien, Odin replied.
Mais oui, this is the drink of the Neudekade,
It reminds me, she continued,
of a Cow I know, who always says *I'm* the Beef!

I've got a friend your Vache would like,
and so might you, Odin reflected—A Long Haul Driver,
Yo Ochenta by name. Most people just call him Joe.
He plies the arid seas between Chicago and San Francisco.
in his beeg reeg named Cacafuego.
I'm about going to punch him in—ought to be headed
right about now for the Cafe Voracious:

Where Overeating
is an Art
not just a Habit

Here's a monomonitor if you want to followem.

Through the cryogenic hiss of the jetspray came now
the microjittery waves of the platinum clad downlink—Hallo Joe!
"O doble" hier!

¡Oiga! ¿Schick Doggie, is that you?

Saluki dropped her monomonitor,
wrinkled the end of her nose and let out
the impressive length of her anima-rouge tongue.
And then she hid her face in the Tan Am magazine.

"O doble" frowned and signaled restraint—
Affirmative, Yo, we're Going to Cheyenne—¿Qui we,
have you divided or what?—¡Pero no!
I just met a hunter. That's it Joe, now we're a Driver,
a Guard and a Hunter—we can take over el Mundo—
¡Claro, efectivamente! Effective when?—When
we get around to it—we'll lay it out in Cheyenne, De paso,
Pero que paso en Wyo?—¿Qien sabe? An Interstate Runs Through It.
Lot to keep track of, glad you're bringin a Hunter—Not
a tracker Joe, her nose is strictly ornamental. We are talken
High Resolution Eyes.
  Es bueno. There's a plenty to see—tráfico Rimbombante.

  The huntress winked and shook her sumptuous ears.
As long as you're getting technical
run him through das Businessenvironment—Who's awake
and Who's nod, What's he seen and Where he's been—
I80, that's the route of the handcarts, Riverbed Alley
just one long Mainstrasse by the sound of it!
  ¿Hear that Yo? By the way, what's your longitude?

  I thought you'd never ask—The Pony Express Station,
sabe the ruins thereof, no longer smoldering,
out my "left-arm suntan window," now I got the hammer down
through Gothenburg, home of the High Plains Goths,
a once warlike people reduced to turning over dry goods—
they could sack themselves if they had the nerve!
And on the shotgun side, overtaking a bedbug hauler:
Longitude One Hundred Degrees West of the Observatory,
and klimben.
  Then Yo Ochenta shifted, supersmooth,
Like an Eel squirmen through a barrel o' KY Jelly.

Phaethon's Daughter

High Plane I-80—

    "Give 'em enough coffee
    and they'll hang themselves."

    Stiff breeze combing the aluminium sky
over the River Πlatte and along the Great Transcendental;
Nebraska splayed out before us like a slab of beef
with the brakes on. The sky filled with the dicks
of little Arab boys raining down like Vienna Sausages—
That's no translation.

       •   •

    Then, from a shaky laser speck on the horizon,
a swarm of Red and Black pokadot Crotchrockets
ratchets into focus and sweeps west toward the umbra
crawling to Omaha in the soft and fuzzy distance—
The lipstikt Sonsubishi, white scarves
trailing a wake of whorehouse perfume
the Gang of 31, harikari into the winde
sixty two wheels on Der Himmel Strasse
winding into *The Truck Stops Here* truckstop.

Phaëthon's daughter Blurr straddles
her Nipponese beast, knees forward in the saddle
like a jockey bound for Hel

"I'll never forgive Satan Bush
for carpet bombing the Garden of Eden—oh allah
I'm gonna cut off your dick
and feed it to the dogs
if you don't strike back—
the world trade center is *not enough*!

"And all the fucking Brazillians
doing drive-bys on their own children
3 generations hunkered on rugs in store fronts
HAS GOT TO STOP!

Abdul Amir Al-Nburi
I salute you and your
Bowlegged, cross-eyed daughter!"

Having discharged her considerable disgust
for the moment Blurr runs her tongue
across her perfect and expensive teeth
and she tightens her classy fingers
inside her top leather glove
and opens the throttle on
her swarm of sonsubishi and continues
lip curled tighter than a slipknot
into the western winde.

       *   *

  The Grain Belt begins its routine, the spacestation
ritual of the wide spot in the road—a game of pool for the argoboys
or der bingo for the particular brainwash of catholics
and indians, ditto bowling for the methodists
and generic protestants
who pray to blow the pins away
down the ball bearing reality of the hardwood lane.
Saturday Night, lit by the tungsten moon
in its time, and witnessed by the rats of the elevators
and patrolled by the prairie dogs along the perifery.

       *   *

  From the cabin in the sky
spread out below the swept alcoa wing
sweeps the vast retrotransit where Mother earth bared
her breast of verdant wheatgrass in irrigated circles,
the irrigating nipples of agrabiz where I-80 skirts and elevates
the fierce little beams of westering traffic
through fields of broken shale
around the shoulders of broken terraces
and over hills of loess laid down
at 500 miles per hour off the face of the ice sheet—
It is quiet out there now—the taste of dog
raised on Friskies, a revolutionary food,

a predator's windfall—the Spam of concocted dogs,
the moral equivalent of chicken soup. But
a dog like that is rarely let out, therefore
such an encounter is deep in the books.
Verisimilitude rules the Dog world. The scent of dog
permeates the cabin, Old Smokers, off the weed for years,
take it in, the original southern, State Narcotic.
Too big to ban: too bad to smoke.

—Denver, 15 Jan. 1995

Radicals on the Great Plain

The Drenchers advocate more water everywhere
whether by silver nitrate dispersal
or by drilling water mining.
They make no distinction between good and bad water
Main enemy: the Dredgers.
Both sexes, however, are reductionist.
The Drieden regard everything with dread,
awe or reverence.
They want to drop the bomb
just to get it over with.
Many members from southern Indiana.
The Dredgers.
They sprinkle flour over everything
and hope for the best.
Large membership from Michigan.
They all live in fear of Polly Decimal,
the queen of the digits.

The Tablewhackers, the spirit summoners
the Pot wallopers, the last of the franchise.
The Tree kickers, anti-ecologenes
who walk through the forest with chain saw tapes
turned on full vol.
The Hole Diggers, a truly lost and aimless
set of brethren related to
the Post setters and Wire stringers.
The head slappers, very indecisive cult.
Never know what to do and so forth.

The Grass hoppers, similar to the
Claim jumpers of the Western mountains,
now largely defunct
But some of their practices are being revived by
The Bankers.
The grass stompers, an alarmist sect related to
the Dirt Stompers, the Dirt Throwers, the Ground Hogs
and Large Land Owners
holding multiples of square miles
a lickspittle sect of

Land Jobbers & Land Grabbers
all under the dioceses of the Bankers.

The Cheese Pairers, a curious but hopeless sect
who hold that out of insignificance
will come greatness, material greatness,
that is, they deem misery and petty economizing
to be honorific.
They are greatly encouraged in this
by the masters of the cult,
the Bankers.
The Bankers
The Bankers live in banks
for the most part this is an advantage
In dry times they just dig deeper into their burroughs
In wet times they are safe
Unless the water,
should the drenchers' prayers be answered,
become so inflated their holes fill in,
in which circumstance
they simply surface and offer them better terms.
Their relationship with God
compared to those who take charismatic chances
seems to be secure
He is rumored to be a holder
of a long-term mortgage.

The Ground Slappers, very short people.
Failing but hoping for the best
and the best will be anything
that isn't definitely awful.
Usually they're the bedrock of the community.
The Weed Pullers, and pullers of all kinds,
prominent among whom are the
the Milkweed Pullers, who are a form of disperser, too
if hapless evangelists.
A certain earnestness characterizes all their endeavors
and among whom
Thistle Grabbers and the Bullet Biters
are impetuous types.
Not to forget their poor brethren
the Knee Bangers and the Elbow Bangers

whose only purpose seems to be
to injure themselves
and who appear to have certain habits in common
with the Folsomites,
an economical organization known for doing anything.

And then there are the Double-Crossers.
an immense congregation who strive in vain
against all the rest, often successfully,
except against
the Bankers and the Whiskey tossers,
descendants of the true Ranchers, still among us
but radically unorganized.

FROM
ROCKY MOUNTAIN SPINE

Montana & Montaner

For Greg Keeler

Big wind, big clouds
Big grass, big rain
Big Road—big load
Big railroad, big caboose

Elk jerky, deer jerky
Jerky de Moose

Big summer real-estate
Long winter outa state
Long water, deep wader
Big Mountain, Big Skiers
Downhill and loose

Deer jerky, elk jerky
Jerky de moose

Designer ranch in the hills
Not far from Big Timber
Incipient and authentic teepeers

Almost the Berserkers
Hook ups, Modern caboose

Cow jerky, turkey jerky
Jerky de goose

Air streamers, day dreamers
Schemers and land jobbers
New age camp robbers
Headed for the calaboose

Elk jerky, antelope jerky
Jerky de moose

Big Dipper bigger here
Little Dipper littler
Horizon infiniter and wider,
Forget the compass—no use

Wapiti jerky, prairie dog jerky
Jerky de moose.

Travel all day, still Montana
Get to Livingston I presume
The County Market and Gil's got it
Gil can keep it—too obtuse

Trout jerky, salmon smokie
Jerky de moose.

Big Militias, pas delicious
Noxon suspicious
Over past Missoula, up above
Flathead, some of 'em dead
Called to their last tattoos

Llama jerky, guinea-hen jerky
Jerky de papoose

Big government: jerky extreme
Sharpshooter waste the dog
Shoot the mama in the door

Baby fall to the floor
Skillethandle Idaho—Megabuse.

Appaloosa jerky, sugarbeet jerky
Jerky de cayoose

Militia Man, Boze Man
Eyes on Ruby Ridge
Randy Weaver, ATF goons
Firepower the federal noose

Rainbow jerky, rattlesnake jerky
Jerky de mongoose

Nye county,
Pie-in-the-sky-county
Except cowpie, i.e.,
Pie in reverse—pie de nuke

Roulette jerky, sucker jerky
Jerky de puke

Good Dog, caretaker Dog
"Drivin' the Boss's Car"
(Hey! Ted or Jane in thar?)
Take'n a chance on a buffalo ranch

Beefalo jerky, merger jerky
Jerky de romance

Big oil, little oil
Stripper wells, swell strippers
Billings motel, bar fights from hell
think I'll pack off to Jordan

Red pepper jerky,
Don't-tread-on-me-jerky—
Jerky de *beg yer pardon.*

Autumn 1995

Denver Upbringing

Down by the Mile High Stadium
Against a car from Elway Motors
the Bikers work a Trucker over
Just to relieve their Denver tedium

I had a bike once—they took it away
They gave me back my knife
Only the other day, but I don't care
I had a Denver upbringing

> *My mom was a crooked cop*
> *My Daddy was a realestate creep*
> *They never even went to bed*
> *And they didn't even sleep*

My daddy said you crazy maniac
you're never gonna wear that
Forty-five when I'm dead
You gonna drive your Grandma's Pontiac—

That's it, your one and only deal
She's sick and she's down in bed!
No way I said—I was outa there
Lit out to Loveland instead

> *My mom was a crooked cop*
> *My Daddy was a realestate creep*
> *They never even went to bed*
> *And they didn't even sleep*

My mom was a crooked cop
And she sent me to jail
She stole from the county
Then she stole from the city

She sent my rings to Arvada
And she took my ruby buckle
She took my SS Special Luger
And she gave it to my uncle

When my mom got the drop
My whole life was a mess
I tore it apart in Loveland
Which is Denver's bastardess

    My mom was a crooked cop
    My Daddy was a realestate creep
    They never even went to bed
    And they didn't even sleep

Well you can have all my rings
And you can take my silver studs
And you can call me screwball
And you can steal my classy duds

But I've had a Denver Upbringing
And you can't take that away from me
And you can't steal my Freedom
Because I never ever *had* any.

FROM
LANGUEDOC VARIORUM: A DEFENSE OF HERESY AND HERETICS

"My country, some few years before the civil wars did rage, was boiling hot with questions concerning the rights of dominion and the obedience due from subjects, the true forerunners of an approaching war . . ."

from Preface to *Philosophical Rudiments*,
Thomas Hobbes

"This leads to bank robberies, murders, decadence and corruption. When a Jew, a pure soul, eats an impure animal, it destroys his soul, and he becomes a jungle man, an evil animal . . . this causes people to leave the homeland and mixed marriages. It's worse than Hitler. McDonald's is contaminating all of Israel and all of the Jewish people."

Yosef Ben Moshe, Meat Inspector in Jerusalem

Jerusalem

The Culmination of the 1st Crusade,
Friday, July 15, 1099

At last the movable towers were constructed.
The wooden towers wheeled to the wall.
From their height the crusaders launched arrows
Into the defenders of the ramparts, the wooden
Drawbridge was let down from the seige-engine
—it was Friday 15 July, 1099, 3pm—
Godfrey of Bouillon strode victorious
Onto the walls of Jerusalem. It had been
Four hundred and sixty years since
The capture of The Citadel by Omar, the great Arab
And the place was now free of the Mohammedan yoke.

The massacre was beyond modern assimilation.

¶ ¶

SUBTEXTS & NAZDAKS
a cruois

¶ English departments from Stanford to Cornell would call the situation of the Serbs in the Balkans a war of "decolonization," except that they've been infected with the term Ethnic Cleansing—who planted that term? Where is the attribution and translation along with the original? This is the result of the "alternative" in which brainwashing replaces thinking based on historic understanding—and it is Slavophobic insofar as most Americans are slavophobes and think the Serbs are the only criminals on the peninsula. This is literally media-generated hatred growing out of a will to extend the Cold Cold War and promote the Croatian fascisti.
¶ Looking back over the tyranny of Rome and Constantinople, heresy is the only honorable mode and response.
¶ State of nature—a war of all against all. If they are in Nature, that's the whole story (or as they now say, "narrative").
¶ Protestant principle—œconomy

† †

TELEFONUS INTERRUPTUS—BREAKFASTUS INTERRUPTUS—MENUMENISCUS LUNCHCHECK—UPCHUCK—DUMP IT—EERIE THEORY UP AN EIGHTH—DREARY THEORY UP A QUARTER—LEERY THEORY UP A HALF—QUEERI UP A QUARTER— DUMP IT QUICK—SPEED OF THOUGHT DOWN A FIFTH—HELMHOLTZ UP AN

No imaginary violence designed to take up
The time of yawning hick audiences with their
Sucker-punch habits and soundtrack bullets
Could remotely approach that day, that hour—
For three days the Crusaders slaughtered the Moslems,
Men, women, children. The Christians
Waded up to their ankles in blood. The Jews
Were burnt in their synagogues.

 Seventy thousand Mohammedans
Were put to the sword. Within days
The infection from the masses of bodies and gore
Produced a wave of pestilence
Biblical in its power and repulsion, yet
Even so, less than the preëmptive AIDS
Of Sodom and way prior to the dark Ebola.
The savagery was Ruandan and Ugandan.

¶ ¶

When you're told to
"think about it!"
Don't think about it,
furthermore, don't
even think about
not thinking about it.

¶ Momentous stretch for religion last week—it was like Chickamauga, like stumbling
past the bodies of the still warm dead. First Donald Davie dies, a truly reconstructed
Protestant soldier. *To Scorch or Freeze* is the most economical rebuke (and that's the
kind it deserves) this age in moral free-fall is likely to get. And Terry Southern, the
greatest of the modern Texas stoics, headed west. And around that time the Lutheran
Prize for Literature announced in Stockholm predictably went to an Irishman of the Ro-
man faith, the only possible entity eligible north of 45 degrees N. latitude in these days of
the resurgence of the Counter Reformation. For several decades the late, great Graham
Greene, otherwise the most obvious candidate, was denied the prize reportedly because

† †

EIGHTH—SIGNAL CONDUCTION MODEST, 50 METERS PER SEC—BRAIN PROCESSES
LIMIT THOUGHT VELOCITY—GET USED TO IT—MECHANICAL MALFUNCTION
RISING—MENTAL DOWN ONE AND THREE QUARTERS—DIMMER DINNER— STALKED
BY CELERY—SELL BY MIDNIGHT—MALFUCTION UP A THIRD—EERIE THEORI

And then, bareheaded and barefoot,
The humble conquerors ascend
The Hill of Calvary, walking in effect
In their final procession,
Loud chorus of anthems from the priests.

Then they kiss the stone which covers
The grave of Jesus, weeping burning tears of joy
And Penitence. This was the fulfillment and vision
Which stayed their course and closed their work.

There were many crusades,
But, like love, none like the First.
Rome has been profoundly visionless
Since that shining hour.

[*Very loosely based on D. H. Lawrence's account in* Movements
in European History *(Humphrey Milford), 1925*]

¶ ¶

he had converted to said dispensation. The worm turns. Beowulf's cloak billows in the
North Winde under a slatecolored sky.
¶ Astonishing news bulletin today—Senator Ted Kennedy has apparently carried a
handful of dust from his martyred brother's grave in the National Cemetery to Jerusa-
lem and mixed it with the soil of the slain Rabin's gravesite—this seems a vast chthonic
insult—this earth was transported in a baggie? on a jet airplane? across the narrow At-
lantic from a land whose State origins were deistic? by a Catholic person who was edu-
cated at Yale? and whose faith is therefore vested in resurrection in the flesh? The wire
service report was actually worse than that, saying he "tossed *dirt* from the graves of
John and Robert." This is Monday, the 6th day of November and disasters rain down all
over the globe. But those are Philippine and natural, and merely to be suffered.
¶ But tell me it isn't true that such conflation of substances, mingling as it were, is any-
thing like the earlier Mormon exposure for having tried to expropriate the dead souls of
the holocaust victims.

† †

RISING—NUTS ON A ROLL—GOODYEAR CONDOM OVERHEAD—CROWD STEADY—
AMBIEN ZOLPIDEM TARTRATE DOWN AND SOMNOLENT—FISH-EYE SHOT—CROWD
DOWN THREE-QUARTERS—HIPFLASK HIPPODROME—MORE DROME THAN HIP—
MESSAGE ON OVERHEAD CONDOM CIRCUM STADIUM—THERE ONCE WAS A KILLER

Bogumil

The Bogomils, the first serious heretics
and the resolute and righteous
foes of the Whore of Rome, believed:

That the Mosaic books were trash
but accepted the Psalms and the Profets.
Also they let stand the four Gospels, the Acts
and the Epistles and included
the Apocalypsus as self-fullfilling.
But they elevated the Gospel of John
above everything, for its pathetic honesty.
And sentimentally they were devoted
to the apocryphal *Ascensio Isaiae*, the "Visio."

Gospel-accounts they took with lots of salt

¶ ¶

¶ The struggle between the three dominant one-god systems has a great deal to do with class and œconomic oppression and very little or nothing to do with religion and theology. And in fact the hierarchs of each system conspire at the top. They show up at one another's funerals and they all participate equally in the satellite auctioning of the public's "privatised" property. The Sheiks of the Gulf have long rendezvoused in the Riviera and the Seychelles, the domain of Romanist dopers and drinkers. And they collect in the floating capitols of transnational capital—it's really the one and only culture. However, the nonempowered just try to get on with their Jihads or the daily reading of the Bible as a realtor's prospectus to the Holy Lands. Unlike the hierarchs, they haven't got theirs, have never had and won't ever have. To them, *"Peace Brother"* is just another exhortation to cease and desist from messy and disruptive attempts to take a little weight off the other end of the balance. Hijack a Concorde with a kitchenknife would be the ultimate lo-tech solution. So it is, so it increaseth. The police proliferate, the prisons multiply. Monotheism grows ever more desperately cruel and bloody and implacable, battering the countless hapless against the stone wall of its singular will.

† †

IN LA / WHO TRIED TO MAKE PHONEINS PAY / THE CUSTOMERS SAID FUCKIT / WE'RE NOT GONNA SUCKIT / WE AINT GONNA PAY NO WAY—900 NUMBERS DOWN A DIME—TALK IS CHEAP, BUT STILL NO TAKERS—PERFECT CRIME WORTHLESS— LIKE ITALIAN BONDS AFTER THE FALL OF MUSSOLINI—POUND (IE EZRA) TAKES A

on the road to the higher facts, and took
the history of Christ to have been
falsified by the Church. They
dismissed the Church hack Chrysostom
and all the other grammerians as Pharisees.

They taught a singular conception of the Trinity—
all three names applying to the father
where in the end the Son and the Spirit flow back
not forward to some corporate jerkus
in a wheelchair—because they held that
even if God was human, the corpus was naught.
There's greek for all this—
They pictured the Father as ancient
(born in Babylon) and the Son
an adolescent, and the Spirit a beardless youth.
Nothing else has stayed so current.

¶ ¶

¶ The violence of a violent Church, now transmitted through a media in thrall to Rome, shifts attention away from Big Resentment of the Organizatzy and the Biznessmen (the priests of Corporation World). The "mafia" is simply the wild (as in sync) subdivision of the corporate state. All of it is "wiseguy fascism" and one of the engines of the rise in the popularity of enforcement—the Church, pulp fiction, fundamentalism, Bill as a lapsed Baptist in a skull cap, you name it—it's the new Catholicism: what to do in Denver when you're dead—which is probably easier than what to do in Denver when you're not dead.

¶ Now that all the Living outnumber all the Dead for the first time in the history of the world, the Living shall Email the Dead. Macintosh, la machina de los muertos, McDonalds controls the nuevo Eucharist of those who are about to die of E coli—Big Mac (carne) and pepsi (sangre). And possibly, in your lifetime, you will see the Dead Emailing the Living, if in fact they're not doing it already (oh no! here cometh Tim Leary) and the Dead will say *kill theeself,* go Kevorkian! it's great here, no skin cancer, no skin, Kaposi no sí, no syndromé, no low fat diet, no race, no ethnic, no acne—don't ask me. The Dead have become the first truly all inclusive, inevitable, no-escape

† †

BATH—GENDER FASCISM UP 90%, INVESTMENT IN POGROM FOR EUROAMERICAN MALES—ACADEMIC MARXISTS STEADY ENTRENTCHED PRICING—REPRESSION OF THE MARKET IN STANDARD WORKS—NAZDAQ PLUNGES, LITERATURE FORCED INTO BANKRUPCY—BURGHERS OF THEORY REPLACE SAMURAIS OF LITERATURE—

Since the mid-10th C.

After that the story gets practical. God's firstborn
they taught, was Satanael,
the highest spiritual being
the universal viceregent.
That position gave him enough pride
to set up his own empire
and recruit a great number of angels.
And as all bankers know, he was cast down
but retaining his creative power,
he set to making a new heaven and new earth.
That's where sundry Protestants
and heretics remain—the parents of God
and the friends of God, and if it comes down
to it, the correctors of God.
They would have agreed with Herr Marx

¶ ¶

plurality. The Dead have finally got something to live for. They work for nothing, they can't
be fired. Hail Dante! Hale Irwin¡

¶ The Virtues are far less interesting than the Sins and therefore far less widely practised.
Putcha condom on, takeya condom off, Sow Bellies down a nickel, palmolive up a dime,
putcha condom in the pouch ov yo sweat shirt for yo bitch, come-on putcha condom on /
come-on putcha condom on.

¶ In 1621 (Plymouth Colony, 1620) George Calvert, Lord Baltimore went out to New-
foundland under a proprietary patent from James I but the climate drove him off and
spared that island from the Roman burden—probably the single instance of the interven-
tion of weather in the salvation of a land. In 1629 he landed at Jamestown with forty
Catholics but the Protestant Virginians made it so warm the Romanists returned to En-
gland and appealed to the as yet unbeheaded Charles I who granted them the feudal state
of Maryland—unreconstructed still, particularly the precincts of Baltimore.

¶ The majority is nearly always against and at odds with the policies, œconomic, so-
cial and political, of the modern monolithic state under whose authority they chafe and

† †

MARKET VALUE OF NEW ISSUE NIL—SELL IT—FEAR AND LOAFING UP A NICKLE—
WIDEN THE RUNWAY—GOOFBALLS STEADY—TAX SHELTER QUOTATION: INTIMI-
DATION BY WIELDING THE DEITY LONG TERM—BUY—GROS CHIEN UP HUIT MILLE
FRANC—PIG HOCKS GLUT THE MARKET—GET OUT—BODY PIERCING UP A QUAR-

who always cut the rules from about thirty to ten.

But the power of the corporate spirit
remained in the hands of the Chairman of Heaven.
Satanael made a new man,
but was able to craft just his body,
it would have been as if a planet of jocks
were to be assaulted by legion after legion
of overweight Shannon Faulkners,
crying without end into the void
and without redemption ever—
until the Apocalypsus, which will ignite
in Extreme southeast South Carolina,
although the heretics couldn't have known that.
But they saw falsifications
along every pathway to the promised land.
From there on it's a fairly straight reading:

¶ ¶

writhe. On those rare occasions—accidental and unavoidable—when they are asked to exercise their will, they invariably say Fuck you, take a Haiku; kick out the faggots and string up the urban criminals. Then it goes to the Supreme Court, Alphonse J. God, Judge. And now, contrary to the Founders' design, Catholics are a clique on that court, galley slaves of Rome, pulling on the oars of faith and submission. The virus of absolute religion replicates in the heart of the assembly, the Roman yoke descendeth once again, to make a joke of the separation of Church and State.

¶ The basic conservative thesis was a simple one. Authority is all of a piece. Question it at one point, and you weaken the whole fabric. Thus Protestantism, which questions the authority of the visible church, is a menace to the whole order of the community, because it sets the private judgement of the individual above the determination of the corporate body>< >> . . . better to accept established error as the truth, rather than run the risk involved in radical reform>< >>Submission to the will of the church was the test of the validity of the prompting spirit>< *The Oxford Martyrs*, A. M. Loades, 1970.

† †

TER—BACTERIA COUNT SHARP INCLINE—VIRUS BURST STEADY—HOLY VIRGIN UP A NICKLE—FRANCESCA DA RIMINI DOWN FOREVER—FEAR AND LOAFING UP A PESO—LESS THAN MINUS ZERO UP NOTHING—SELF-FLAGELLATION ON THE RISE— GUILT AND SELF RECRIMINATION UP ONE AND A QUARTER, GILT UP AN EDGE—

Satanael seduces Eve and Cain becomes
their gift to the race, prevailing over Abel
their own child, Moses was the agent
and promoter of Cain and the inheritor
of the Power, but when Jesus showed himself
after the resurrection Satanael gave up
his angelic syllable el *and became Satan*—
Just another victim of downsizing,
all his power transferred to the Sufferer.

This was preference pure and simple—
which we've suffered these two millennia.
No thanks to the Intermediarie's
æons of wasted time, to terminate
the Christian Era, a direct but degenerate
extension of Imperial Rome, Fascisti
with Wizard of Oz routines
and KKK regalia and get-up.

¶¶

¶ Ορτηοδοξια is the character of a right-thinking person, society, school of thought or
Church. The Kaiser said "I hate the Slavs—I know that is wrong, one should hate no one,
but I can't help it . . . the thing to do now is to get every gun in readiness in the Balkans
to shoot against the Slavs." Can't give a source on that, it's from memory. On July 28, '14
Austria declared war on Serbia. The same day the Turks (what was left of the Øttoman
hegemony) asked Germany for a secret pact against Russia. In Arkansas they were squeez-
ing chickenshit between their toes like they are now. The banality of the choice of Day-
ton, Ohio to debate the problem of what the French call trés Balkan (meaning hopeless)
will be impossible to top. The slavophobia left over in the refrigerator of the past ten cen-
turies is a fuel supply as large as the oel said to underlie their strife-born peninsula.
¶ The Austro/Hungarian Empire walks again, another, futile Roman campaign to re-
claim the summer palace of Trajan. The Kaiser also said of the scandalous, crumbling,
decrepit, penniless Turks, given to misrule and corruption, "Under no circumstances at
all can we afford to turn them away." Germany today sends its Roman shock troops to
support Islam against the Ørthodox.

†††

ABUSE UP SHARPLY—EXCUSE UP THREE-QUARTERS—GET RID OF IT—NAIL THE
BOSS TO THE CROSS—CONFESS AND THEN ACCUSE—TRASH IT—JUNK IT—SELL
IT—PUMP IT OR JUMP IT OR DUMP IT BUT DON'T HUMP IT—INFECTION ON THE
RISE—LANGUE D'OÏ SPLIT, SADIC DIVIDEND—OUR MOTHER'S CATHEDRAL DEVILS

Shoko

5,500 persons injured in reprisal
for the Americanization of Japan

Some dissenters disagree somewhat
Other dissenters object
Rather more than not
But the great chiliastic heretic, Shoko Asahara*
Disagrees a lot.

---

* Chizuo Matsumoto, his abandoned name

¶ ¶

¶ The old Constantinople is still the enemy here, the schism into right and wrong. The right being "on the right" or the Right church and on the left, or wrong church, the Roman, self-evolved church. Long before the Cold Cold War it was taken for gospel that the fight between Berlin and Moscow paralleled Rome and Constantinople, simply moved north. And that the totalitarianism common to both the Church and its putative enemy Communism, was driven by the engines of dogma.

¶ What do you think? It is possible that the Germans will get in on the pros- ecuting side of the war-crimes trials shaping up for the end of the Millennium and coterminously the end of the most self-righteously self-serving self-justifying self-vindicating self current century. It seems inevitable.

¶ A German judge will try a Jewish convert to Orthodoxy for the summary execution of a Mohammedan Believer. Or a thousand. Spencer Tracy won't be there to supply celluloid indignation this time around. There will be no indignation for the Serb—the Muhammadan Yoke has been hitched to the Roman Yoke and strapped to the neck of the Orthodox.

† †

IN STONE—OBSCENE CARVINGS IN THE MISERÈRE STALLS, HOLY GHOST REVELA-
TIONS MERGER ANNOUNCED—DEVILETTES BUGGERING GOING GOING—UP—
DOWN—UP—DOWN—UP—DOWN TOWN—OPTIMISM BIG AS A HYAENA'S CLIT—THE
MARKET TRÈS BALKAN—BONDS FOR WAR ON ISLAM CONVERTED TO MASSA-

Tomás Torquemada—first Inquisitor General for all Spanish Πossessions and Master of the rooting out of disbelievers.

"To the people, all religions were equally true.
To the philosopher, all religions were equally false.
And to the State, all religions were equally useful."

Edward Gibbon,
The Decline and Fall of the Roman Empire

The Inquisitor-General:

the life and effects of Torquemada
Nephew of Juan de Torquemada—Turrecremata en Valladolid,
translated into the new world of Yucatan a city of freaks,
dwarfs with splayed limbs, withered membranes,
eyes polished over with pearly deficiencies, endemic scabs
and crooked bones, all the psychic horror of the New World
cpmfrpmtatopm (ie., confrontation)

¶ ¶

¶ Nazdaq *stock Intellectuelle* takes a dive——cant and jargon on the rise, fed by the pap of opportunism——since when was hard luck ingenuity not a legitimate free market skam: 25 year old "woman" (right out of Melville's *Confidence Man*) poses as 13 year old boy abandoned just before the Christian Holiday Grande in Salt Lake City bus station, the City of the Saints, father dying of AIDS, the plague of the Cross par excellence, the modern torture from Aragon, the biomechanism Torquemada wouldn't have dared dream of in the wildest desperation of his Spanish peninsula mountain night sweats, even as the crown's Italian agent plied the sea of wingéd snakes beyond the western boundaries of Atlantis, Plato's right wing, central control hedge against poetry (altho there would be precious little of that sent back with the Gold and Silver destined to feed the raw Christian avarice of the Sixteenth Century, the moral Inquisition emanating from the yacht and the roman bath and the jet propulsion Concord's quick transit of the narrow Atlantic, reconnecting Europa's worst, most thrillingly awful promises to the Red Man's Real Estate, and the rock personality's subsequent spreading of the new trans-species plagues of VD, powered by the final decades of the 2nd

† †

CRE OF THE ORTHODOX—ARMS STOCKS ADVANCE—BUT OPTIMISM FLAT—LANGUE D'OC, TECHNICAL TRICKS SURGE AHEAD—MERRIMENT AVEC INVECTIVE UP AND AWAY—BUY SHORT—HOLD—RYDER RENTAL TRUCKS UP, WAY UP, ALL THE WAY UP, OVER THE TOP—SELL—DUMP—LIQUIDATE—NEW MESSAGE ON

crashing and bleeding out on the shores of a freako
azteko bloody interlude between beauty and heaven
bleeding out into the gutters and borders where all comers
regardless of gender are waiting anxiously for their period;
the stress of birth and living without the aid of virus—
and note! here in the definitive state of America that stress
is *the* New World ailment—all shipped this was
across the narrow Atlantic, over the far resultant
& murky entanglements of Jean Rhys's sea
by Tomás Torquemada, the very first of the moderns—
greater than his near contemporary,

Because Niccoló Machiavelli's articulation
of the sophisticated evils of state craft are more complex
and more difficult to acquire than the techniques of torture,
which are quickly mastered by persons whose
only special talent would be a perverse imagination, a thing

¶ ¶

millennium's throes, the thrown rods of its killer psychochemical engines, Japanese re-
search torture and metropolitan rape and German eugenic incineration.
¶ Polish Popish Mendel, peas and recombinant construction of the disease-free, World
Person, the post-African rectal dilation and electric moment of the penial dependency,
orgasm without end or issue, only as product, creatures of a corporate god at last. A cool
low and fitting end to the second millennium: a bus station, a woman acting the role of a
puberty boy with a tale of abandonment in a society where the scam is more interesting
and accurate and sociologically authentic than the actual case—Utah! This tale couldn't
have happened to a bigger bunch of hypocrites.
¶ A Business passing itself off as a religion objecting to an honest con artist. Shame. They
should give her a decent farm and several husbands, and reverse their stupidly wealth-ridden
Polygamy with a little real functional Polyandry. Not likely. Watch the NAZDAQ for the in-
crease in price of Coca Cola shares, sans the coca; the longest standing fraud in soft drinks.
¶ The brotherhood and the sisterhood emerged from the presumably less sentient

† †

GOODYEAR CONDOM CIRCUM OVERHEAD: THERE ONCE WAS A JURY IN LA / WHO
SAID NOLO'VICTED, NOLO PAY / HE'S YOUR N WORD NOW / BUT HE'S OUR SACRED
COW / SO GET THE FUCK OUTA THE WAY!—NAZDAQ SUMMARY JUDGEMENT UP FIVE
AND THREE-EIGHTHS—TRADE IN ROPE BREAKS CEILING—SUBMISSION ON THE

so widespread as to be common, but also,
there's the dark probability that the willingness
to inflict systematic and progressive pain
is genetically transmitted—how else are some few
naturally better at it—but the studies are too appalling to cite.

¡Hail Torquemada! Saint Πain! utterly neglected
in the pantheon of the great professional providers of suffering.
So that, all the more cheated
is He who knew and practised the most.

Tomás Torquemada became the tutor and the confessor
of Isabella, the infanta, when she was eight, when
her mother took her regularly to Segovia.
He was then Prior of the convent of Santa Cruz.
This was around 1430 of the Christian time—already
Torquemada had refused the highest theological degrees

¶ ¶

great hunters, but their impulse is certainly still present among the gross apes from the
corporations who maintain their fly-in hunting lodges in the Lake of the Woods and in
Neil Young's North Ontario but more importantly Walt Whitman's Blue Ontario's Shores,
the funds stolen from the pensions of the ignorant dwindling toilers still lucky enough to
have a retirement account to be sacked.
¶ This is the impediment the fundamentalists stand against. To cross over and cast their lot
with the clever and speculating and evil apes is their great fear and hesitation. But of course,
they are enlightened compared to the progressives, who assume that they must administer
to those who have been forbidden by their God to submit to the argument that they are just
an extension of the apes of the Leakeys and the Heart of Darkness. Kentucky, Tennessee,
the Carolinas, southern Illinois to lower Mississippi, forget Alabama, from Brecht to von
Braun—those plantations will never be beat into submission. They are impervious to engi-
neering because they already have a culture extending from the 17th century, like the
transplanted Africans who they understand, and with whom they sympathize.
¶ The imported, cultureless and now useless masses of the industrial wastes of the old

† †

RISE—DRASTIC MEASURE TO MAINTAIN ORDER, MASS AND RANDOM EXECUTIONS—
PANIC IN THE PRISON-BUILDING LOBBY, DOWN A NICKLE—OVER-PRICED HUTS,
OVER-AMPED NUTS, SILICONIZED BUTTS GAINERS—PUTCHA CONDOM ON, THE
NEW LEG-FLASK, SMOKELESS ROOMS FULL OF CALISTOGA, PISS IN IT, POUR IT

out of disdain for earthly advancement. And in fact

this great Dominican was the truest Dog
the Lord ever had, because he exacted from Isabella
the fateful and famous promise that she
would make it her principal business, when she ruled,
to chastise and destroy heretics—so saith Esprit Flechier,
bishop of Nîmes—and thus was planted the seed
of the greatest humiliation since the torture of Christ,
and the most exacting instruction ever rendered
on the political advantages of religious submission,
and the preparation for that most tremendous engine
any state ever had at its disposal anywhere: the Spanish Inquisition—
and altho certainly that adjective goes without saying,
we must remember and never ever forget,
the fact and operation of said righteous torture
is the envy of the Irish, the Poles, the Israelis,

¶ ¶

Union, the great interior northern drainage, the relatively high wage, plentifully fed and clothed, mobile, and in Veblen's sense invidiously programmed proletariat, well, they've basically been cashiered. If the industrial revolution was born in Birmingham and Manchester, it died in Cleveland and Toledo. At least Ned Ludd was recognized as and paid the respect due to a visionary who saw in one flash the end of basic human endeavor, and the creation of Malthusian lemmings streaming in mammalian waves to the cliffs of despair and destruction—born to live and die in chronic hunger, threatened without pause, never knowing rest, infected by physical and psychic discomforts and the constant barrage of the warring elements and by the corporate state offered a cheap and empty longevity, demeaning and contemptuous and dispensed. Utah. Utah will be known as the surviving gallery of Dante's exemplary rogues, a desert hell in a business paradise. Hail! Birdie Jo Hoaks, wherever you be.
¶ Where are the Barbarians at the gate now that we need them to dismember and waste this decadent power? They are nowhere to be found. The current arrivals are not Carlo Trescas—no way, Au Contraire, these End of the Second Millennium Types only

† †

BACK IN THE CALISTOGA—PALMOLIVE UP ONE AND A QUARTER—DREADED WINTER, FULL OF RAPING CANADIENNES—MODERN AS A POST: SHIP THE JOBS ABROAD, PUTEM OUTA WORK B/C THAT'S ALL THEY GOT. FIRST (16TH C.) SEPARATE ŒCON AND ETHICS, AND THEN GET RID OF THE ETHICS—GROS CHIENS ADVANCING

and probably the Albanians—and this list
leaves out Vodoun and chicken blood and cigar smoke.

Tomás Torquemada invented the modern
and the post modern world—and set the style
for the future application of violence.
Because the nerve centers are fixt, electricity only
effects the mode, not the phenomenology—
and another thing: the world habit of deploring the practise
yet supporting the regime is older than diplomacy.

And so Isabella was the destined backer,
created out of Torquemada's genius
for torture in the venture capital enterprise
known as the discovery of the Americas.
All that kicking against the scapegoat Columbus
in the terminus of the millenium

¶ ¶

want to invest in it. Attila is on NPR, with promotional think pieces on how bad the Anglo
Saxons are; when it comes to Race, repulsion is always reciprocal. The fact is, the human
race is not a bunch of monkeys beating their meat in the trees, they're on the ground killing
each other and enjoying it.
¶ The big secret everybody keeps is that murder feels good. That must be why it has the great-
est proscription against it, although like every act in the present clime, the stricture weakens,
and the punishment grows slack from indifference and simple lack of accommodation.
¶ The Cold Cold War slid into new campaigns against the drug trade and the systematic
isolation and exposure of the poverty-stricken, a sort of reverse infanticide, the ancient prac-
tise of exposure and abandonment. But that was always a necessity dictated by supply and
the exigencies of the hunting and gathering life. The modern way is to stare at it, and when
the light changes, step on the gas.
¶ Slap a tail on those monkeys, fish a few out of the garbage scows, bestow upon them a
sandwich if they pray and stay sober, and so force them to contemplate and witness their
awful relegation.

† †

ON THE SINGAPORE INDEX, PREMIUMS ON MONKEY BRAINS, UVE AND QUIVER-
ING AT THE TABLE—GOURMET FAR EAST MONKEYS UP A QUATAH—WITTERUNGS-
VERHÄLTNISSE WORSEN, DARK NAZDAQ—WESTWARD HAUT—I AM NO GREEK,
QUOTED—THE BEARS YAWN, THE BULLS DALLY WITH THE FIXERS—SPORZANDO

was just further superfluous proof
that the boatloads of subsequent fools
dispatched to do the dirty work still don't understand
they were nothing more than a pitiful riddance.

¶ ¶

¶ Criminals are given shelter, food, heat, drugs, sex, dumbbells, phone calls and a possible future beyond the walls; it's cushy. The random danger, the exposure to the diseases of the body and the mind are probably not that different from the vicissitudes of an ordinary life outside. It's a living.

¶ The Counter Reformation was driven to wrest back the control lost in Luther's rebellion, to reassert the power of Mediterranean autocracy, derived from the fixed structure of the clan and the blood rites of the brotherhood. Now "brother" is a mere salutation, like the kiss of death, and extended families of unrelated people in teepees have replaced the clans. Interventionism flogs the general population and proliferates false accusation, it foments chronic resentment and instills a nightmare gestalt in the animal preserves of the urban wilderness.

¶ The Bozniaks perpetuate war between the schismatic churches; the dissenting ghosts of Bogomilism assume the outward yoke of Islam and throw in with the Turks rather than submit to a God who keeps accounts, on two sets of books at that. Occident and Orient.

¶ In Stalin's letters to Molotov (immortalized in name by the greatest, most egalitarian

† †

SHADOW BOXES WITH RUINATION—OPTIMISM TAKES IT ON THE CHIN, TRUST AND RESOLUTION IN STEEP DECLINE—ROGUE, INC., (THEORY SOFTWARE) LAUNCHES HOSTILE BID FOR EUROLIT—TRASH AND PULP MIXED WITH VITRIOL FLOOD THE MARKET, COMPETE WITH FERTILIZER AS EXPLOSIVE NEWS ONLY IN THE MIND OF

Notes on Béziers: the past as cauchemar

Simon de Montfort moves down the Rhône
into the sea fog across the marshes of Roussillon
and then relentlessly onto the Languedoc plain,
his destination the Eglise de la Madelaine
and the Cathedral de Saint Nazaire.

Arriving at the north bank of the River Orb
the twenty second of July in the very bloody year
twelve hundred and nine following
the Judeao-Roman scapegoating
and capital torture of the Messiah, the awful

Simon, Count of Montfort: nephew and heir
of Earl Robert, created by King John
Earl of Leicester, a cité he never

¶ ¶

cocktail ever made, the perfect instrument of purification in the geopolitical epoch of the combustion engine) he rails against the Interventionists, the bourgeois specialists and argued that they should be made to confess publicly and recant their attempts to divert concentration on the revolution into irrelevant social designs of their own, like elevating workers from the bench. In another guise and manifestation Stalin would have made an excellent, corrective President of Stanford (not serious and not commensurate). He was also rather more than Republican on the state budget, saying that it should be in surplus and no more currency issued. Early proto-IMF ideology.

¶ He would have no problem dealing with Bill and Hill and their Serbophobic policy in the Balkans—Nato in charge of child abuse and ethnicity, the armies of the peace-keeping righteous rounding up the south Slavs of their choice, Cold War II in which the Austro-Hungarian Empire now launches guided air to surface missiles and tools through town in Humvees, camouflage clone uniforms replace the comic opera costumes of Emperor. But this population is too mixed and the terrain too forested to be carpet bombed.

† †

THE ACADEMY—FANTASY UP SEVEN EIGHTHS—RESULTS OF PROCEDURALS YIELD
THE FOLLOWING: ATF SCHOCKTRUPPS BADLY IN NEED OF INSTRUCTION IN
EMOTIONAL AWARENESS, SELF-CONTROL AND NON-INCENDIARY CONFLICT
RESOLUTION—SANCTIMONY SOARS—INVENTER OF BLACK HOLES FINDS ©OD—

so much as visited, a piece of luck
for that country bumpkin town.

This petty lord of the Isle de France
was directly solicited by Innocent III
(preëmptive name, no?)
to root out and exterminate
the heretics, who were as thick as ticks
on the body of the Roman Church of Septimania,
for which service he could keep all he seized
over the whole course of the punitive expedition.

This was an inducement custom fit
for a creature of such legendary pettiness
gross avarice and proven venality
and indicates the Pope's canniness
in a time greed &c was virtually

¶ ¶

¶ Two tendencies have always defined the policy of the German Tribes—their rivalry
with Rome and their attempt to replace the New Testament with a blonde body builder,
while Rome installs a Greek shipping magnate mythos to account for archaic privilege.
¶ The lumpen Arkansawd Baptist Bourgeoisie Jumped-Up by Yale Alias for revolution-
glia, Ha!
¶ Long before 1209, the Cathars were fully convinced of their perfection and they had
demonstrated by total abandonment to love in practice and by total doubt in theory that
the Church was just a collection agency levying protection in the usual Italian way, i.e.,
"Give me a hundred dollars a month or I'll kill ya." But this was the beginning of French
Voluntarism ending finally in the Buonapartes and the Pantheon, now including the
Church of the Curies who were killed by X-ray, not radium.
¶ As the present voice cannot speak of such things because honesty has long been a
categorical heresy against the modern state the parallels for Simon's tremendous op-
portunism would be difficult to assess now—and then there is the incalculable

† †

PIETY GOES THROUGH THE ROOF—BOGOMILS NOT AT TABLE IN DAYTON—
NEGOTIATIONS FOUNDER ON OLDEST DILEMMA OF LES BALKANS: INNATE HATRED
BETWEEN THE RELIGIOUS FACTIONS «RECONCILIATION» (WHICH NEVER WORKS)
TAKES A DIVE—THERE ONCE WAS A KILLER CELL / KNOWN AS THE CELL FROM HELL—

the only pursuit licensed by the Church.

As the ground fog clears and lays the dew
the cathedral mass if emerges over the Orb
and from its depths comes the murmer
of the twenty thousand quaking souls,
the Cathars stoic with certainty
their Catholic friends and protectors
worrying their surplices to tatters
with the magic sign of the cross, all
gathered in the colon of the mother church
packed and trembling together waiting
to be evacuated to eternity
for they have had the news of the advance
of this professionally bloody force
under the bizzarely cold Simon de Montfort.

¶ ¶

influence, supremely modern, of *making a virtue of the inevitable*. Still, the main features
were exposed by the Reformation, the revolution which cannot speak its name, and are
automatically applied to the Serbs by a fast-food glutted and vaticanized, self-professed,
wannabe Jesuit Arky like Bill, who forks over his Baptist lessons to the last bellicose exten-
sion of Rome/Boston.
¶ Religious tolerance is the surest sign of belief in nothing, nihilismus, the club lunch.
Once capital enterprise was pried from the stone grasp of the Roman administration and
its financial agents, Protestant capitalists lined up toward the Roman magnet like iron
filings dressed in business suits, the replacement habit of hierarchical control. It was the
"population" of the reformationist countries who got thrown to the dogs, the new Do-
minicans who finally came to be the Big Dogs of international biz and promoters of the
new "reformation" aka multiculturalism, the cult par excellence of late imperialism. But
that's quite Roman too. Rome was the first clearing house culture, the ascendancy of the
disciplined horde populations over the northern races who were left to bear the cold and
difficult singularities of individualism (the "you're on your own"

† †

GOODYEAR CONDOM CIRCUMS DOWNTOWN CLEVELAND, MISTAKEN FOR AKRON,
DROPS TONS OF SPERM PELLETS ON ROCK HALL OF FAME, NO EFFECT—FAME FLAT,
ANONYMITY ADVANCES—CHRISSIE HYNDE, BOB LEWIS, JERRY AND THE PACEMAK-
ERS, THE MOTHERSBAUGHS, STEADY AS FIRESTONES—FORGET THE BROWNS, JIM

This Massacre and cremation
is the occasion and the moment
of the justly famous generalization
uttered by Innocent III's secretary
when asked how the faithful
were to be discriminated
from the disbelievers:
"Burn them all! for the Lord
  will know his own"
came the reply from the Emissary
of Absolute Authority.

¶ ¶

plank or the Swiss Heresy), which was never about direct access (the propaganda) to God,
but to the vaults or the crypts, where the bones of succession wrapped in the titles are
kept. Joseph de Maistre, the most vehement and toxic and interesting despiser of the Ref-
ormation and champion of the Counter-Reformation makes this same point for entirely
different purposes than herein deployed.
¶ Thus the surplus numbers shipped out to the west by the North were by definition aso-
cial outcast wanderers (not Dante's) and radically unlike the blessed and yoked and cultur-
ally programed hordes of Mediterraneans and Iberians, the <Dark White> cradle Romans
[usage reintroduced here from H.G. Wells, *Outline of History,* Garden City, 1949.]

† †

BROWNS GONE ANYWAY—DEAD AYN RAND STILL PULLING THE STRINGS OF GOV-
ERNMENT WITH HER MARIONETTE ALAN GREENSPAN—INTELLECTUAL MAR-
KET SUFERS SEVERE DROP—STILL UP FROM 87 WHEN MICHAEL JACKSON'S AND
TED TURNER'S ADVISOR STRIPPED THE REPUBLIC OF IT'S PILFERED ASSETS——

Albi, a Day Trip

Albi crawls today
with the narrow-eyed descendants,
the compliant bad tempered offspring
of the first inquisition into
deific rebellion, the sign
of Manichean indifference
in the face of centralized authority
and the overweening enthusiasm
for success even if it requires
the total cartoonization of sentience
and the squandering of perception
who even today look like
they're waiting for somebody
to cough up some Protestants,
so they can get on with the business
they made their reputation on—
Market gardening, public dining,
national conversation concerning
the scandal of the bourgeois results
of Roman ambition and culture,
dynasties replacing royalty, a sop
thrown to a demos dedicated
to endless somnambulent lunch
in preparation for a dinner of pigeons
and rabbits and snails and tubers
filled with ascospores, rooted out
by trained pigs; but now synthesized
by the ever questing copycat Japanese.

The hotels are always full in Albi,
just because they say they are.
The supplicants for shelter grow mad
with anxiety, they've been to the church,
which was designed to brutalize
the senses, an immense sign of power
and preëmptive caution, an orange light
which a little less than a thousand years
will fade to yellow, as the traffic
and sheer mobility and pollution
weaken all intensity of vision

and dillute the expeditionary fever
with the sheer rush of aimlessness
and the revelation
that destination would have no meaning
even if it existed, producing
a species-wide despair
and a generalized intuition that life
is a colony, workers and drones
managers and armies, queens
passing eggs on their thrones,

Procuring perpetual conferences—
but you know it's just still
the Inquisition, booked up, forever
persuading or dismissing the heretical
barbecuing the truly insistent,
pulling apart, an inch at a time
the uncertain, since, if they
can reason enough to be unsure
a visitation from the devil is presumed.

Ville d'Albi. From across the Tarn
Cathedral mass of Saint-Cecilia
looms, the farthest reach of Rome,
now ruling on the cheap, with
the threat of moveable courts
and the force of unexplainable events,
the power walk way to heaven
fed by the farming of the heretics
roasted by fire, hell brought back
into the here and the now,
the only place and the only time.

Cathar comes from the Greek
meaning pure—they rejected
all food which was produced
from animal intercourse. They
abhorred the sacraments of the Church
bread, wine and water
for they saw in such veneration
the raising up of the material
realm of Satan, the old and only bargain

and that, in fact, Caesar,
who at least had the decency to show up
was now replaced by a cheap
bunch of spongers in robes
claiming to have the ear of God.
What the Cathari witnessed
and sensibly rejected
was the replacement of an organized
disciplined military caste
by a bribing, whoring, and disease spreading
ecclesiastical administration—
nobody's ever called that an improvement
and they were the direct antecedents
of our present inspectorate,
overseeing our accounts
conducting our audits
stamping our paper,
seizing our children, death drugging
our heretics, electro-shocking
the perfecti, rat conditioning
the mutate minorities, the mouth
foaming fieldmice streaming
from the vast estates
of the Oligarchies to the south,
conquest by breeding and spermdumping.

The bottom line of that great,
degenerating power is
Bad times get Worse, so
don't expect much, and be grateful
for the occasional porc chop—
our bereavement is universal
but transitory, it's not
exactly pie in the sky—
it's more like a bagel, with
a cross instead of a hole. I
believe in the Virgin Mary
says the Devil (minor CEO),
and then takes down his pants
and defecates on the trolley, just around
dinner time, on a first class flight
to Whereverdad. Central America.

Albi. I'll be, You'll be, Al'll be.
Eventually we'll all be. The thought enforcers
grow stronger, their gain is post-expotential—
it gets along without potential, it runs on decay
The main faux-fortress church is set in the centre
way above the Tarn, gross, intentional,
as threatening as a stationary object
can be—a machine,
an even higher form of administration.
It was there from the beginning.

                The Inquisition:
the founding of the modern state. No doubt.
The new corporate buyout of the Empire
occurred in Albi, after the first decade
after the first great burnings
by Montfort—
Still all that's nothing
to the incineration of Béziers.

But atmosphere is not made up of details—
Albi is Albi today as it was
In 1220 anno domini.

        By rejecting all that, the heretics
unwittingly showed the way
to the end of the millennium
where the Imperial conveniences
transmogrify into culture
and demand privilege on the grounds
that they have been denied (abused)
—Like, not unreasonably, the Inquisition
happened to *Them*—
and morally lacerated by the schism
and the theft of church goods
and ground, and so turns the Mass
into the mass. Dumb and Clever.

Rome owes considerable
back-rent on the Reformation.

Do the Simon de Montfort /
Do le Busard

Qui frappe'n sur la porte?!

C'est moi, c'est moi
Simon de Montfort!

O non! O non!
Ce n'est pas Simon de Montfort?!

Si! Si! C'est moi, c'est moi
Simon de Montfort,
Levez-vous la porte!

O non! O non!
C'est Simon de Montfort—
Vite! Vite!
Fermez la porte!
C'est le busard, Simon de Montfort!

Mais non! Demandez la porte!
C'est moi, Simon de Montfort!
Ouvrez la porte, ouvrez la porte!
C'est moi, Simon de Montfort!

Simon de Montfort? Vraiment?

Simon de Montfort—oui!

O non! O non! Le Busard!
Téléphonez à la gendarmerie!
Vite vite, tout de suite!
Téléphonez à la gendarmerie!

Ten Years in Gaul

Religious wars are the only real wars
they're gods' wars
The true ground of ordeal
and fervor, brought on
To concentrate the faith
And to set fire in the spirit.

Cold wars are fought over territory
Or over minerals and materials,
Control of licenses and rights
To hold leases from afar,
To displace, exile and banish
To capture and enslave populations.
All with business in mind.

Word reaches us the Helvetians
Are loading their luggage
to cross the Rhine.

The Corporation, above reckoning,
Spreading Misery and pestilence,
Transporting cholera under pressure
Landing and dumping the bacterium
The cultural carbuncles of its cargo.

Causing attrition of sentience
Throughout the market
Through satiety with cheap goods,

The endless baubles of science
And the progress of grotesque medicines.

Rome was certainly a corporation
In the year 58 B.C., when Caesar
Gave free reign to the plebeians
And rode off toward Geneva,
Covering 700 miles in a week
On horseback, beating the Popemobile
on its own, struggling with every stone.

Dismissal

The Greatest Poet of this expendable century
was also its greatest, most public Heretic.
He made anti-Semitism a heresy,
although he wasn't the greatest anti-Semite of his time.
Or even close.

A Modern gang of cutthroats
in cartoon berets, with sumo champions
like Gertrude Stein—
The giant abbreviator from Oak Park
who wrote, stuttering
pseudo-wise hymns to war, and
its effects on the adventurous sector
of the lower/upper middle class.

The Anti-trial

The hearing of arraignment
has been described elsewhere.

He was detained not because
he was the Greatest Poet,
they couldn't have known that anyway
nor would they have given a hoot
far from it.

There was no trial because everybody
knew it would be a witch trial—
an actual, sticks-around-a-post burning.
It was too historic, too soon after
great upheaval between the Europeans
and the cast-offs of the Europeans. Besides,
insanity is the ultimate dismissal!

It was too familiar, a fitting end
to the old, uniformed fascism of the two wars
gliding into the transpace of the new
hierarchical oriental fascism of beehive
conformity, industry devoted only to survival

and ruinous increase. Singularity,
the swamping of the gene swamp.

  All of it fondly called
the Modern Movement by those
who fervently hope it is over
and that their banal attempt
to get rid of a whole period
by driving a stake through it
will finally give them an end
to their belaboring the scapegoat.

On the Question of God's Tolerance

The question is intolerable—
The Lord is everywhere.
At the pagan banquet, at the orgy
In the lethal bacterium of the bath,
And in the stringent puritanisms
Which pervade the general war
Against nature and all her wanton works.

The Lord is Everywhere.
It is the Lord who deviseth the drive-by.
This is the Lord's TV, The Lord
Likes primitive social games.
If there were a foursome of Lords
The streets would be their fairway,
But there is only One Lord.

And He is not amused by golf, except
Occasionally when he runs lightning bolts
Through the ground into the punter's spikes
And they wilt suddenly and fall over
Like daisies, their heads hitting the ground,
Their clubs scattering, their carts close by,
Mute chariots, witnesses to their whimsical end.

The Lord is not only tolerant, but obliging,
And complicity is not in the question—
Complicit with whom? Some bystander?
Does anyone imagine the Lord

Seeks ratings? Blood and bread,
Altar and victim, terrorist and terrorized
And everything nonconformist
Is written on the palm of The Lord.

The Lord is everywhere. Truly,
The Lord deviseth the drive-by
With the weird haircut driving,

As well as the nullification of gun control.
The Lord inhabits the heretic's explosion
Permeates its rage and resentment.

Jehovah is The Lord's hand puppet.

Off-the-Books in Darien

Meanwhile, in the Fourth World,
In this century of counterfeit freedom,
After the lime is scattered on the surface
After the paraffin is poured in the pit
And the rotting feet, infected bone of peons
Marching in place through the dead of night
Stamping out the vintage where the slums begin
Where the red dresses and shoes of the whores
Congregate around their priests
On the high corners of urbana,
Those who wait for Ali's Justice wait in vain
Because there is no breach in the traffic
Engineered by off-the-books profits
Of the false prophets of Christ, where
The Ethos of the State and the Ethos of the Church
And the Ethos of the Traffic cross, which
Constitute the Cross and the evil of secret power
Conveyed by the Bishops of misery and supply
Arriving nightly in their opaline windowed Limousines
Still reflecting the eternally white peaks
Strung along the distant Andes like beads.

Corsica

Long deep harbor perfect for sea robbers
and banditos from classical times
limed with steps on sheer stone walls
twelve kilometers from Sardaigne
across an island dotted strait now
said to be infested with mafia yachts

Odysseus's instinct wisely kept him back
from entering this attractive shelter—
seeing no ploughed fields or other
signs of human activity, catching sight
only of whisps of smoke rising from upcountry
a scouting party was cooked on sticks

By the Laestrygonians who came
running in their thousands at the news
more like giants than men, possibly Archaics
probably descendent from the neolithic dolmen
carvers, whose sites lie in the cork oak forests
hidden in the hills to the north.

All the ramparts are now lined with restaurants
and the water has turned to Heineken
but no danger from the interior now
or the stone throwing maneaters—
the pirates own the nightspots and the harbour
and run the trips to Grotte Napoléon on the hour.

Petra Kelly—recalling German Green, 1992

When Petra Kelly shot herself
I was right beside her in my heart
and my admiration for her steadfastness
was complete and totally unlike
what I feel for the black-boy whips of McDonna
or the earlier pretenders like Jane and Joan,
in the brief history of corrective sensibility.
      The careful mediation of her
American accent, the pure Georgetown
german weltwaves in the background.
      Certainment, why hang around
for the land to fill up with genetically resentful and
overproduced Southerners just so the pretenders
can get their carpets vacd?
      The history of the world has been written
with the disappearing ink of those accounts
and the pilfered wages of their solution—
the sine qua non of population dumping.

      ¡Salute! and so long Petra.
For the price of a single round, you ducked
the destiny you described, and gave the colour to,
and framed—the born prophet
of a finale full of Fall Out,—Bye Bye.

Mordecai

Mordecai Vanunu was the most brilliant Israeli.
He was the merest, secret whizz
in what's left of the conscience of the wilderness.
Well named for Mordecai Day (Purim),
the celebration of Spring over the destructive forces of Winter
and the rainy season, The Fallout,
and the dark night of radiation, so says my Hastings.

First they hounded him in London, and they
ferreted out his weakness with an irresistible
sexo-sensational woman—they're like
the Russians in that way,
they really know how to run women. Indeed
he followed her like a frothing dog, dripping the foam
of hydrophilic submission right into the planeseat
to Rome and then on to Tel Aviv. And the Mondo Press
slavered too, for all the world wanted to know the route
Mordecai took to his eternal incarceration.

He would have been thinking of *Blowup*
when he slapped the window of the van
with the ballpoint message on his hand—
patty cake on the paddy wagon,
as it rolled him into Sinai oblivion.

And when the film was developed and blown up
it revealed the whole secret archive and picture
of everybody who'd made the bomb from Chicago
to Moscow
with the metaphor on the palm of his hand—
Hail Mordecai! the most brilliant of the Israelites.

[October, 1986]

Sniper on the Roof: the cheap elimination of heretics

The equipment has a certain cost—
the supertech Remington Police Rifle.
The training is laid on by the Central Force
for those eager to kill, but not just to kill,
no, to kill a human, from say 90 meters,
a man, not a woman no, no, not a woman,
not even a worthy man, but a trash man, drunk,
emotionally distraught, unable to see a way,
black probably, but even better, white—black—
black is too obvious, too recurrent,
too easy, too repetitive, too predictable
too apt to generate confirming statistics,
and affecting a part of the white population
who don't care a whit about a loser
whiteman getting gunned down for,
apparently, the amusement of the media.

North American dogs get more respect
than the man raving with family trouble
at the sun in the day or at the moon by night.
No jail time, no room and board on the county
no rent due for putative privatized prison space,
this is population control, pest control
straight out, no more thought to charges
than would be due rats in their subterranean
urban towns,

                Some of this mankilling
is called suicide in the "officer do your duty" style
utterly ignorant of the sniper lurking on the roof
waiting for the signal, the checkered flag
signaling the start of the frozen race to eternity.
Cheap beyond the imaging power of the target
this is not so cheap as doctor death's plastic bag,
true, but then this is state murder, not
the legal, struggle between a pathologist
and a pathological state, this is not big fauna
sought by rich men, this is not the wrack
above the fireplace, this is the old wrack across

the back of the inquisition, only now
there isn't even a question before the answer.

But the Mexican or other Meso-americans
in the crosshairs too much resemble
shooting dogs streaming across the border,
a chain loop in a carnival, alien culture,
cinco de mayo, the day of the dead, muerto
built into every gesture, a waste of ammo,
and in fact demeaning to the sniper. This is
palpable desperation, this targeted man
doesn't have a computer, or even a primitive
weapon, this man's hunter is Raytheon of course
via killer personnel in full swat combat dress.
fresh from an Abudabi arms fair. Every
jerkwater police force will apply for the grant
of a state sniper who can eliminate
the non-cooperative, those who are now
the public nuisance, the epidemic of just
plain trash, to be picked up, put on the stretcher
and hauled away to the dump of postmodern
American madness by the lackeys picking up
after the Central Force—anyone with
good eye test and a steady finger and
no conscience whatsoever at all can apply.

Tribe

My tribe came from struggling labor
Depression South Eastern Illinois
Just before the southern hills start
To roll toward the coal country
Where the east/west morainal ridges
Of Wisconsin trash pile up
At the bottom of the prairie, socially
A far midwest recrudescence of Appalachia
My grandfather French Quebecois
Master pipefittter in the age of steam
Indian fifty percent, very French
Who didn't derogate himself
As a breed, showed none of those tedious
Tendentious tendencies. Came down
From Chebanse, from the Illinois Central
In Iroquois County, to the Chicago &
Eastern Illinois line's division at Villa Grove
In one of the Twenties boomlets,
The last precipitous edges of the great devolvement

These forebears on my mother's side
Owned a nice clapboard house in old town

Where I was brought up off and on during
The intensity of the depression, parents
Wandering work search, up and down
The bleak grit avenues of Flint, following
Other exodus relatives, Belgian in-laws
From another French connexion
Michael Moore-land from the beginning
Manmade poisons in the cattle feed way
Before Creutzfeldt-Jacob disease and angry cows—
Governments always conspire against
The population and often
This is not even malice;
Just nothing better to do.

I'm with the Kurds and the Serbs and the Iraqis
And every defiant nation this jerk
Ethnic crazy country bombs—
World leaders can claim
What they want about terror,
As they wholesale helicopters
To the torturers—
              But I'm straight out
Of my tribe from my great grandma Merton
Pure Kentucky English—it would take more paper
Than I'll ever have to express how justified I feel.

Sketches from Edgewater

Thin sheet-ice on Sloan's lake
"dark white" shine, late February sun

Big red balloon tethered over Cub Food
winterpale shoppers, struggling with the load

like overweight ants dragging their take
away from an abandoned sandwich

A long ghost-white buick idles at the zebra
black glass, chrome gone, white tires

A deal in every aisle, every hour, every day
says a colossal signboard on the vast hanger

Trenchtown plays over Calliope's system,
to incredibly naive shoppers, just musac

Automatic misters drenching the leafy veg
lots of root food, caros, manioc, cocohuitl

and exotic tamarind shells and subtropical fruit
Bob Marley whispering ethiopian over all the aisles

Immense bins of hard candy, hills of choc drops
individually wrapped, stacks and stacks of snacks

Twenty-five yard long strips of freezers full of Stouffers
which should smell like cat-puke if the power gets cut

As in the Gulf War, when Iraqis had to throw
thawed food to the dogs who soon got fat and ran in packs

like the customers, maybe, in Edgewater
if it ever got bombed and the power got cut

Idle comparisons at the checkout
cash only, bag your own, Alaska style

Just then a zippy old man drives his cart up—
"Alzheimer's Alzheimer's, I think I got it!"

I tried not to look at him, thinking I might catch it
he smiled and winking, turned to the checkout girl

"Sheila, my dear, the girl of my dreams"
Sheila smiled, displaying nice dimples in her full cheeks

He was really charged now—"See this?"
he swept a copy of *People Magazine* from the rack

On the cover is an outrageously famous star
modelling a bikini—"That's my wife!"

Sheila shook with laughter, "Alzheimer's Alzheimer's,"
he hummed "I think I got it." Then, a change of firing

in his temporal lobes, set off a sweet
and very passable rendition of *You're My Everything*

I liked it, Sheila liked it and the old man
sung while he put his scant fare on the belt

Outside again, the sun was higher than a shopper
on sugar and fat, and the lot was aswarm,

drivers bearing away their dietary burdens
all backdropped beyond the lake

by the powerful agnostical structures of Denver
optically far away it seemed, but O, so near.

February 1996

The Drugs Are Over-rated

The drugs are way over-priced, but
they are scripted and dispensed
as if they're ambrosia,
which as far as I can see
is a very peculiarly American
stupidity, mention morphine
which is designed to put you
asleep and the whole DEA
pharmacopoeia swoons in self-
adulatory self-righteousness, why?
Who knows, because they are
known lovers of pain, for others.

Oh my dear auditor, how can I put this?
The drugs are very bad,
but more refined than civilian drugs
the "dope" from which
the agencies draw their unholy levies,
their off-the-books war loot,
that seized money they pay the dogs.
Well, the dogs don't actually get it
but they get the love returned by the trainers
their sniffer skills are theirs forever
along with the presumed habits
which keep them on the sniff!

Tylox can put you out there for a while—
relief from generalized pain.
Vicodin seeks the street, a pilfered bottle
here or there, which is a poor comment
on the cold forlorn rue, paved
by the engineering state. And then,
there's Atavan, Shelley Winters says
makes her life wonderful, which is O.K.
but way low on Wonder. If it is wonder
ye seek knock on the door of a wizard
not the hollow counter
of the pharmacist at Rite Aid.

Infusion Day

On Infusion Day
every thing comes back.
The big fat lady who will
never learn to use a needle
even if she has a line of my
kind a thousand miles long,
and then,
the voices of the unburied dead
and the satisfied symphony
of the truly dead,
along with the secret lurking
of the pure internal marks,
the passage of the pure week—
life turned into a seminar.
The periodic bruise,
the exiting of the blood to work,
the cell count, the inventory
of the shelf life, meaning
the life of the shelf, the tear count
the involuntary drip account
the measure of the mystery of what
remains of the life and times
of the victim, condemned but not delivered,
just the keeper of the count, slowly
joining the counter.

Chemo du Jour: The Impeachment on Decadron

On being offered a room of my own,
the chance to take some notes,
a television/VCR unit, some hot chocolate,
peanut butter crackers, sure, why not,
looking over the common room I'd heard that
collection of testimony—I opted for isolation—
a temporary suspension of my Mass Observation duties
and the chance to look over my recent notes
from Rome and to brood on the pallor
of the Spanish Steps and the moist brow
of Keats's struggle to die, still palpable, almost
visible through the window of his somber room.

"... a week passed and two more days, and John
knew his dying day had come, yet to achieve death
might be a day's hard labour. Severn held him
as if carrying him to the gate ... To put off the world
outside—the children's cries, snatches of song,
a cheeping sparrow ... the sun streaking the door ...
a bigger problem was to separate
himself from his body— ..."*

The butterfly needle. The nurse patting the vein,
searching for a wall to carry the load of Decadron.
Decadron sharpens the senses
around the optic nerve and the neocortex,
enabling one to see through walls and into
the present—there goes the Pope, mobile as ever—
there goes the king home from Sloane Kettering
(yes of course it's Mayo, the mayonnaise private pets)
to stave off a coup, then to be buried by a squadron of pilots
all wearing the same café Bohème headgear
and into the immediate past,
as the drip is connected to the pump I see W. J. Clinton
full humping St. Monicka panting in the pantry
I see D.C. people walking like negative ghosts

---

* from *Abba Abba* by Anthony Burgess, Faber & Faber, London, 1977, p. 82. Work suggested by Tom Clark after author's trip to Rome.

past the Casa Blanca,
I see the public petty ire as a bomb
in the garbage scow, sanctuary to an aborted
human baby, neo-natal trash from this trash social
structure, the product of the policy of Billy & Hilly,
this fetal thing wrapped like pisces in a copy
of the *Washington Post*, the voice of Babylon,
they wish, but instead nothing but
another methane burner
in a swamp of overpaid busybodies.

I see the slogan FORGIVENESS graffiti style
on the dirty side of the scow, I see Black African
American drive up in the Volvo disposal truck
and commence to onload the pizza engorged scow.
I see now FORGIVENESS crossed out and *Repentance*
scrawled below and that crossed off
and REMORSEFULNESS replace it before
my tightening optic nerve. The Nurse brings
more Carnation Hot Chocolate, Nestles rises
to the surface of the Third World pooling
over my brow, *yea* I am super into the steroidal
cognition of Decadron—this must be why athletes
do so much steriodal, to enhance their vision,
and their mammoth paycheck, and the graffiti-like scrawl
proclaiming MISERY rises to the surface of my cocoa,
and floats off on a raft of bubbles and lo, the Africans
drive off into the prozac shrouds of D.C.
past the security gate—through the window,
past the guard shack, hard by
the dim, futile unreality of the pantry.

And then, dear, sweet Bill and Santa Monica
give up the struggle to uncouple
and with a shrug go at it again. The saline drip,
bridging the chasm to Taxus*, Latin for the yew
bridges the chasm of my senses. The conductor
to the ionic connexion, which produces

---

* Pactitaxel, the brand name of the chemical derived from the yew tree bark—note the
 bizarre Nahuatl aspect of the word.

the violent interface at the holy war
of the short haired puritans with
the screamers and shouters
and yellers and scoffers and pushers
of the *media res*—acquittal?! Forget *Acquittal*
or quitting of any kind—"I entered,
but I never came."

        Yet *behold!* I see W.J.
light up a beeg Stogy from Havana Viejo
and take a call from a Congress person,
while receiving joint rejuvenation from below.

I see him in the Taxol pooling over my brow
move his arky hand from the arm rest
to the Iraqi button and then my
supercharged vision bends and stabilizes
an image of a white woman's severe
and Germanic demeanor in the Senate Well
Harold Ickes lied I see graffiti-like on the back
of the Volvogarbage collector vehicle plus
a list of renowned same-sex freaks whose names
cannot even be uttered.
The unit ponderously passes through the securigate
and way beyond, reflected in the surface
image collector of the steroid, the curvature of the earth
from the obscure Islet of Diego Garcia East of
the Arabian Peninsula an experimental
missile vibrates and flames and then launches
from the carrier, and Oh Good Lord, minutes later,
as the nurse strips away the Medusan tubes of my oncology,
American dumb missile arrives with punity
in the southern suburbs of Baghdad, ruined Cradle of Civilization,
just north of the Garden of Eden which looks, I must say,
rather abused and tacky now that Bill has had his way—
in the Celestial Light of public approval
And Lo now the Taxol infusion clears the atmosphere
where I see the Superbowl completely superseded
by the *superblow*, O yes, praise the Tree Lord,
now it is time to go.

The Dull Relief of General Pain—
Oxycontin, Roxicodone and Codeine
in General

If hundreds of thousands, perhaps
millions of people in North Korea
are succumbing to starvation,
if eighty-five percent of the country's children
are malnourished, and in some towns
corpses line the streets and rumors of
cannibalism are rife, where's Bob Geldof?—
are these people not the world?
Are they too late on the world's stage?
Doesn't Michael Jackson like children anymore?
Or did he never like communist children?
What's going on? This is poetry calling!
Poetry is waiting for an answer.

17 January 1999

The Decadron, Tagamit, Benadryl and Taxol Cocktail Party of 1 March 1999

Weighed in at 144, slight loss
Anglo Saxon measure of about ten lbs.
underweight but on the gain
so I wished upon a star
not about where you are, not about.

I'm wearing new Ariats
with a machine sewn fringe
the latest Chinese arrogance,
cowboy boots—indeed—
they're light, and might account for
the missing pound,
the missing pound of flesh.

Blood pressure normal to perfect
as usual. My tumor is watching all this.
My tumor is hearing all this. My tumor
is interested in what interests me, and
she detests who and what I detest.
My tumor is not interested in what
or who I love,
My tumor is not interested in love,
no neoplasm is—the blind cells thereof
are not interested in love or affection,
she sends out little colonies, chipped genes
mark their crossing the river, they are
without variation, they keep time with terror.

She's like Wittgenstein's lunch, utterly invariable,
and, she's like your own private third world
she arrives and breeds like guinea pigs,
evermore progeny and evermore food
and the priest cells
demand evermore progeny and then
they all demand independence and this

is in Your territory. But then I see her
puzzled misapprehension and know
what she can never anticipate when my spirit
will watch this Bitch burn at my deliverance
in the furnace of my joyful cremation.

White Rabbit

The bloodworker was in a bad mood
unreasonable as it would be
to imagine she enjoys her work
if she enjoys hurting you as
an aspect of not enjoying her work—
well, I'll have to interview the alien
on that one. Sometimes I imagine it yawns.
Life for an alien is not any better
than it is for the subject. This fact
is rarely remarked.

The drawing method they use at this clinic
is a spring-loaded blade which slits
the side of the great or the ring finger
very fast, very painful but very brief
mercifully, sweet baby Jesus, *very* brief.
The bloodworker extracts the blood
with a series of short passes
over the slit,
the blood collects in the rounded
bottom of a small test tube.

Why do it this way rather than
sticking you with another needle?
Exactly, yet another needle
the whole affair is an attack on the veins
to get *at* the Alien and its migrating colonies.
Cancer is Catholic—it loves to
evangelize, and it will intermarry with anything
to claim the progeny.
I suppose I made a smart remark
as usual, my tongue has been
my genius and my downfall.
The nurse began to collect the specimen
with ever increasing pressure on the split flesh
I nearly fainted, but not a tear
fell from my lid, and not a throb shook my throat
until I'd left the collecting station
and then I shook and wept, and Jesus,

I'm sorry to say I hated that
bloodworker even despite the fact
that I knew she couldn't help
what she had a great irresistable
need to do, to hurt me deeply
because I was a bearer of cancer.

We had saluted the day when
Jenny said WHITE RABBIT.*
I lay for a while trying to think
what would I wish for if such a genie
really delivered—a dismissal of the alien?
. . . no. There are wishes too complex to be granted.
I wished (and I'm not supposed to tell you this!)
I wished for a needle worker to
set up my infusion lines
without blowing a vein.
And lo and behold, into the
waiting room came a nurse
like on a half shell
except dressed in white
and led me to a small room
with a TV/video cassette port
which I'd never reached before.
Flawless butterfly insertion
uncomplicated, competent anchoring
I could have wept at my good fortune
but I didn't, I thanked her
sincerely and asked for a V-8 juice,
I was even drinking it without enzymes.

And soon my vision tightened with Decadron
the first of the drips instilling you
with the fortitude to take the onslaught
of the now looming Taxol before
the sleepy-*Alice-in-Wonderland*
admixture of Benadryl and stomach
stiller Tagamet, oh wondrous day

---

* On the first of the month you make a silent wish upon awakening—the first words out
of your mouth must be "White Rabbit".

Chemo day, Monday, and it must be
obvious to all in this era, obvious to all
telling the truth violates
your right to free speech
violates your expectation of credibility
and downright violates your plausibility
and your sanctity.
Telling the truth will greatly amuse your alien
if you got one.

The Invasion of the 2nd Lumbar Region

They came in spaceships
the size (i.e. dimension)
doesn't matter
smaller than matter
no matter—submatter—
less than those breathlessly
small particles the
media bombardment
are always squawking about

2

A lone crow
on the high wire
flies north
crossing the first
skylight north
and then arc'd low
crosses the 2nd
flight now
skimming the bottom
edge of the frame
of time, the reminder

3

Torn loose from
the human fabric,
adrift in the human breeze

20 October 1999

The Garden of the White Rose

Lord, your mercy is stretched so thin
to accommodate the need
of the trembling earth—
How can I solicit even
a particle of it
for the relief of my singularity
the single White Rose
across the garden will
return next year
identical to your faith—
the White Rose, whose
house is light against the
threatening darkness.

BIBLIOGRAPHY

Selected Publications: Poetry

The Newly Fallen, Totem-Corinth, New York City, 1962.

Hands Up!, Totem-Corinth, New York City, 1963.

From Gloucester Out, Matrix Press, London, 1964.

Geography, Fulcrum Press, London, 1965.

Idaho Out, Fulcrum Press, London, 1965.

North Atlantic Turbine, Fulcrum Press, London, 1967.

Gunslinger, Book I, Black Sparrow Press, Los Angeles, 1968.

Gunslinger, Book II, Black Sparrow Press, Los Angeles, 1969.

Twenty-four Love Songs, Frontier Press, West Newbury, MA, 1969.

The Cycle, Frontier Press, West Newbury, MA, 1970.

Songs: Set Two, a Short Count, Frontier Press, West Newbury, MA, 1970.

Gunslinger, Book III, The Winterbook, Frontier Press, West Newbury, MA, 1971.

Recollections of Gran Apachería, Turtle Island Foundation, Berkeley, 1974.

Collected Gunslinger (with Book IV), Wingbow Press, Berkeley, 1974.

Collected Poems, 1956–1975, Four Seasons Foundation, Bolinas, CA, 1975.

Manchester Square (with Jennifer Dunbar), Permanent Press, London, 1975.

Hello, La Jolla, Wingbow Press, Berkeley, 1978.

Selected Poems, Grey Fox Press, Bolinas, CA, 1978.

Yellow Lola, Cadmus Editions, Santa Barbara, CA, 1981.

Captain Jack's Chaps—Houston/MLA, Black Mesa Press, Madison, WI, 1983.

Collected Poems, 1956–1983, 3rd Enlarged Edition, Four Seasons Press, San Francisco, 1984.

From *ABHORRENCES*, Limberlost Press, Boise, ID, 1989.

Gunslinger, 2nd Edition, with Intro. by Marjorie Perloff, Duke University Press, Durham, NC, and London, 1989.

ABHORRENCES, Black Sparrow Press, Santa Rosa, CA, 1990.

The Denver Landing, Uprising Press, Buffalo, NY, 1993.

High West Rendezvous, Etruscan Books, Buckfastleigh, South Devonshire, England, 1997.

Chemo Sábe, Limberlost Press, Boise, ID, 2001.

Way More West: New & Selected Poems, edited by Michael Rothenberg, Penguin, New York, 2007.

Selected Publications: Prose, Fiction & Essay

What I See in the Maximus Poems, Migrant Press, Ventura, CA, 1960.

Rites of Passage, Frontier Press, Buffalo, NY, 1965.

By the Sound, Frontier Press, West Newbury, MA, 1969.

The Shoshoneans, Wm. Morrow & Co., New York City, 1966.

Some Business Recently Transacted in the White World, Frontier Press, West Newbury, MA, 1971.

The Poet, The People, The Spirit, Talonbooks, Vancouver, 1976.

Roadtesting the Language: An Interview with Ed Dorn, by Steve Fredman, UC, San Diego, 1978.

Interviews, Four Seasons Press, San Francisco, 1980.

Views, Four Seasons Press, San Francisco, 1980.

By the Sound, New Edition with Intro. by author, Black Sparrow Press, Santa Rosa, CA, 1991.

Way West: Stories, Essays and Verse Accounts 1963–1993, Black Sparrow Press, Santa Rosa, CA, 1993.

EdDorn Live, edited by Joe Richey, University of Michigan Press, Fall, 2007.

Translations (With Gordon Brotherston)

Our Word: Guerilla Poems from Latin America, Jonathan Cape/Goliard, London, 1968.

Tree Between Two Walls by José Emilio Pacheco, Black Sparrow Press, 1971.

Caesar Vallejo, Penguin, London, 1975.

Image of the New World (from Yucatecan & Nahuatl), Thames & Hudson, London, 1979.

The Sun Unwound, Original Texts from Occupied America, North Atlantic Press, Berkeley, 1999.

Recordings

The North Atlantic Turbine, Fulcrum Press Records, London, 1967.
Gunslinger Books I, II & The Cycle, S Press Tapes, Munich, 1970.
Satiric Verses, Alternative Radio, Boulder, CO, 2001.

Critical Studies on Edward Dorn

Beach, Christopher. *ABC of Influence: Ezra Pound and the Remaking of American Poetic Tradition.* University of California Press, 1992 (Chapter 9, "Migrating Voices in the Poetry of Edward Dorn").

Clark, Tom. *A World of Difference: Edward Dorn.* North Atlantic Press, Berkeley, 2002.

"*Edward Dorn.*" *Sagetrieb,* Special Issue, Vol. 15, No. 3, Orono, ME, 1996 (1998).

"Edward Dorn, American Heretic," *Chicago Review,* Summer 2004.

Elmborg, James K. "*A Pageant of Its Time*": *Edward Dorn's Slinger and the Sixties. Studies in Modern Poetry,* Vol. 6, Peter Lang Publishing, New York, 1998.

Fox, Willard. *Robert Creeley, Edward Dorn, and Robert Duncan: A Reference Guide* (an annotated bibliography). G. K Hall & Co., Boston, 1989.

McPheron, William. *Edward Dorn.* Western Writers Series #85, Boise State University, 1989.

Sherman, Paul. *The Lost America of Love: Rereading Robert Creeley, Edward Dorn, and Robert Duncan.* Louisiana State University Press, Baton Rouge & London, 1981.

Streeter, David. *A Bibliography of Ed Dorn.* Phoenix Bookshop, New York, 1974.

Wesling, Donald, ed. *Internal Resistances: The Poetry of Ed Dorn.* University of California Press, Berkeley, Los Angeles, & London, 1985.

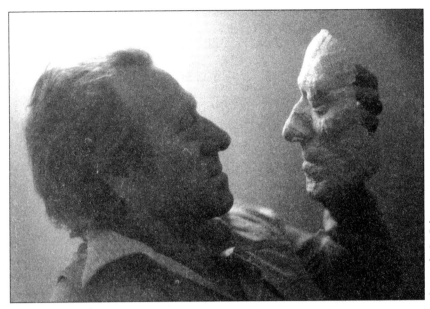

photo credit: Ira Cohen

Edward Dorn was born in the prairie town of Villa Grove, Illinois, on April 2, 1929, in the wake of the Depression and grew up in rural poverty. He never knew his father. His mother's father, a railroad man, was French Quebecois, with Indian ancestry. His grandmother was "pure Kentucky English." He attended a one-room schoolhouse and in high school "played billiards with the local undertaker for a dime a point, away from school weeks on end," until an English teacher convinced him to get an education. A visiting Scots Methodist preacher, who had the intellectual honesty to say that "everything is not going to be okay," further inspired him, but after two years at the University of Illinois, he dropped out. He was working at a tractor factory in Illinois when "a set of circumstances and warps of destiny" took him to Black Mountain in 1951: "I was educated at the University of Illinois, and somewhat corrected at Black Mountain College."

Under the tutelage of Charles Olson, whose *A Bibliography on America for Ed Dorn* set up the methodology for his future reading on the West, and with Robert Creeley as his examiner, he graduated in 1955, having taken off for three years to travel the West, hitching rides, seeking work where he could find it, and returning with a wife, Helene Buck, and three children. After leaving Black Mountain, he continued this peripatetic wandering across the transmountain West, following the winds of writing and employment from San Francisco to Bellingham, Washington (the setting for his autobiographical novel *By the Sound*, which depicts his marginalized existence in the "basement stratum" of society) to Santa Fe. In 1961 he accepted his first teaching job, at the University of Idaho in Pocatello, and the following year his first book of poems, *The Newly Fallen*, was published by LeRoi Jones' Totem Press. He spent the summer of 1965 visiting Indian reservations with the photographer Leroy Lucas for their collaborative work *The Shoshoneans*, and in the fall he joined the newly created department of literature at the University of Essex in England, as a Fulbright lecturer. He spent most of the next five years in England, where he published several collections of poems and wrote the first book of his masterpiece *Gunslinger*. He also collaborated with Latin Americanist Gordon Brotherston on translations of "guerilla" poems, and met his second wife, Jennifer Dunbar.

He spent the '70s as an academic migrant, teaching at Northeastern Illinois University in Chicago, Kent State, Ohio University, the University of Kansas, the University of California at Riverside and at San Diego, and the University of Essex. In San Francisco he collaborated with the printer and artist team Holbrook Teter and Michael Myers on a series of surreal and subversive projects, including the newspaper *Bean News* and the publication of *Gran Apachería*. In 1978 he accepted a professorship at the University of Colorado, Boulder, where, with Peter Michelson and Jennifer Dunbar Dorn, he edited the more substantial *Rolling Stock* magazine throughout the '80s. During the '90s he taught at the Paul-Valéry University in Montpelier in the south of France, from where he made expeditions to the hilltop fortresses of the Cathars—the heretics of *Languedoc Variorum*. He was also working on another long poem, *Westward Haut*, and after he was diagnosed with pancreatic cancer in May 1997, the poems for *Chemo Sábe*. He continued teaching at the University of Colorado and giving readings of his work in Great Britain and Europe, as well as in the United States, until his death on December 10, 1999.

PENGUIN POETS